Ben Drew

*To Capt Mac
from one fighter pilot
to another
all the best
Urban Drew*

Property of "Mac" McNciol
Rancho Bernardo CA 92128

URBAN "Ben" DREW
UNITED STATES ARMY AIR FORCE

Ben Drew

The Katzenjammer Ace

R. R. Powell with U.L. Drew

Writer's Showcase
San Jose New York Lincoln Shanghai

Ben Drew
The Katzenjammer Ace

All Rights Reserved © 2001 by R. R. Powell

No part of this book may be reproduced or transmitted in any form or by any means, graphic, electronic, or mechanical, including photocopying, recording, taping, or by any information storage retrieval system, without the permission in writing from the publisher.

Writer's Showcase
an imprint of iUniverse, Inc.

For information address:
iUniverse, Inc.
5220 S. 16th St., Suite 200
Lincoln, NE 68512
www.iuniverse.com

ISBN: 0-595-20638-7

Printed in the United States of America

This book is dedicated to the 53,000 airmen
in the mighty Eighth who never came home.

Contents

Foreword xi
Preface xiii
Introduction xv
1 ACHMER October 7, 1944 1
2 DETROIT 1941 3
3 NASHVILLE Cadet Days 7
4 TUSCALOOSA Flying at last 11
5 MISSISSIPPI The Potato Patch 16
6 MALDEN, MO In Trouble Again 24
7 MARIANNA ...who you know. 28
8 LEIPHEIM First Flight 30
9 BARTOW No Navigation 34
10 BOTTISHAM It's a Long Way to Tipperary 43
11 TOUSSUS-LE NOBLE First Time 58
12 LISIEAUX First in the Air 63
13 FRANCE Bogey 67
14 BOTTISHAM II Katzenjammer 72
15 CAMBRIDGESHIRE The Bottisham Four 76
16 GERMANY Horrido 81
17 ALPS Postcard 89
18 CHARTRES No Ammo 92
19 THE ENGLISH CHANNEL Dull Duty 98
20 WITMUND The Bleeder 102
21 ROSTOCK One versus One 109
22 BOTTISHAM III Promotion 116
23 LITTLE WALDEN September Song 124
24 BALTIC SEA Monster Boat 130

25 FRANCE Mistake?	134
26 HAMM First Encounter	139
27 ACHMER Shooting Swallows	147
28 RHEINE Wingman Down	158
29 ACHMER II Misfortunes	170
30 GOUROCK Homeward Bound	177
31 FRöHLICHE WEIHNACHTEN Christmas 1944	182
32 WILMINGTON Thunderbolt	189
33 EUROPE No Fighting	196
34 PACIFIC Cows and a Crossing	201
35 IWO JIMA Hot Rock	206
36 SAIPAN Bureaucracy Bungles	214
36 MICHIGAN A.N.G.	219
37 AFRICA One War Was Over	224
38 PRETORIA Award	228
39 WIESBADEN Hospital	232
Chapter Notes	243
Glossary	249
Katzenjammer Kids	253
Index	255
About the Author	259
About the Artist	261

List of Illustrations

1. Ben Drew dressed for combat. i
2. Drew as an instructor at Bartow. 42
3. The officers of 375th Fighter Squadron 55
4. Bill Kemp dressed for combat. 66
5. The Bottisham Four 77
6. Eder with Me-109 84
7. Leutnant Georg-Peter Eder with mascot. 86
8. After Chartres 96
9. Col. J.J. Christian 97
10. Bill Kemp and damage 106
11. Detroit Miss 117
12. Betty Lee II..119
13. Kemp gets three 129
14. Blohm and Voss BV-238 133
15. Me-262 Unpainted 141
16. Sergeant Cruikshank and Lieutenant Drew 157
17. McCandliss ID Papers 167
18. Me-262 Under Tow 176
19. LtCol Kruzel..179
20. Katzenjammer Kids 180
21. Drew and Crew Chief..181
22. Party Table 218
23. Drew Award 231
24. Drew and Eder 235

Foreword

When I asked Bob Powell to write the history of my military career, I knew he was a good author. It wasn't until I read the manuscript for the first time that I realized just how excellent he was. This book is unlike any other book written about fighter aces or fighter pilots. It is unique in its approach, unique in its style, and magnificent in its content. The treatment of my story by bringing in the names of Eder, McCandliss and others, makes the story much more readable and gives the coverage a wider perspective. The story of my missions over Europe and my one mission in the Pacific theater is well treated by Powell. He has managed to write in such a manner that the reader will be totally enchanted. It is unlike any other book ever written on a fighter ace. He has told my stories, the good and the bad. He has not enlarged on them nor has he held back on incidents which to some would be embarrassing. I congratulate him and feel sure the reader will as well.

In looking back on those years where at the age of twenty I was leading men into combat, it is difficult to realize what I accomplished at such a young age. What we did in those days will never be repeated. There will probably never be another fighter ace in aerial combat.

Urban L. Drew
San Diego, California
June, 1998

Preface

This is more than the story of one man's adventures during World War Two. After I first met Ben Drew in 1979, I knew I wanted to tell his story. As I wrote, I discovered that to tell his story, it was necessary to tell other stories as well. This minimized the multiple "I" and "Me" usually found in fighter pilot memoirs. Soon there was a cast of characters as if it were a novel.

It is not, however, fiction. What you are about to read is as true as I can make it. If it were only numbers and dates, simple facts, the story would make lean reading. In filling out details, creating conversations, I have deliberately overstepped the bounds of the academic historian. I call it "True Memories" as opposed to "Factual History". I have added a section of Chapter Notes to specify artistic speculations as well as facts that remain unresolved. Even the literary embellishment is as appropriate as possible to the time and circumstances. I want readers to feel that they were there.

Besides deciding whether "True Memories" or "Factual History" was the more accurate description of this book, I also had problems with what type of narrative it is. Conversations with Ben were obviously the major source of information, but there were other interviews, memoirs, documents and book research, so I finally decided it falls between biography and auto-biography with a dose of old fashioned story telling.

I hope you enjoy the story, I certainly enjoyed writing it.

R.R.Powell
Virginia Beach
May, 1998

Introduction

I am pleased to have the chance to do a second edition of the Ben Drew book. Besides the obvious errors that seem to sneak by into any publication, many people have called or written and submitted changes and additions to this bit of history. Contact with the veterans of the war, people who were there, has not only been interesting, but an honor for me. The interest *Katzenjammer Ace* generated has been gratifying. The subject of World War Two and, particularly, the war in the air seems of great interest to today's readers.

Not all contributions were definitive and there still are conflicting viewpoints. Controversies remain. My plea for additional information, therefore, also remains. If you know of related events, additional facts or would simply like to share your thoughts, please contact me at one of the addresses listed in the back of this book.

However, above all, I hope this revision will be even more enjoyable to read and will add to the recorded history of that period.

R.R. "Boom" Powell
Virginia Beach, VA
August 2001

1

ACHMER

October 7, 1944

The roar of the departing jet fighters had barely stilled when a pair of yellow nosed P-51 *Mustangs* flashed over the trees. The bellow of their engines followed. They were going 450 miles per hour as they crossed the end of the runway at Achmer. Ahead of them, the wheels of two new *Messerschmitt 262s* of the *Kommando Nowotny* smoothed into their flat bellies as the jets climbed after take-off.

Pulsed puffs of white smoke blew back from the leading *Mustang's* gun ports. The trailing *Messerschmitt* exploded in black smoke, red and yellow flame. Pieces of airplane and fire fell to the ground as the *Mustangs* flew over.

The first *Messerschmitt* was accelerating. It banked to the left and began a sweeping turn. The *Mustang* banked further, turned harder. In the cockpit, First Lieutenant Ben Drew fought to bring his gunsight pipper on to the fleeing jet. The high airspeed made his control stick hard to move. G forces pulled at him. His arms and head grew heavy. He was grunting rather than breathing.

The glowing orange pipper was on the dark green jet. Now he had to pull the aiming dot ahead, along the flight path. He had to pull lead — allow for his bullets' flight time and drop. The *G's* increased. The edges of his vision became gray, but his aim was steady. Hours of practice, months of experience were behind his shooting. He squeezed the trigger and the six fifty caliber machine guns of the *Detroit Miss* fired for the second time. He held the trigger down.

The *Detroit Miss* was a P-51D *Mustang*. Like her sisters in the Three-sixty-first Fighter Group, she was mostly shiny aluminum. Her nose and spinner were painted yellow to a back-slanting line behind the exhaust pipes. Her name was painted in white on a long, red bomb shape on the left side of the nose. Wingtips, rudder top and canopy edge were also red. Elaborate Nazi flags were stenciled in black and white on the red canopy edge – there were five.

Sparks along the *Messerschmitt's* fuselage showed where the bullets struck. The deadly sparkles crept forward. The clear canopy flew off the *Messerschmitt*. Ben stopped firing. The German jet flopped on to its back and spun into the ground. The explosion was loud and colorful.

German jet airdromes were heavily defended. The airfield at Achmer had had no warning of the attack. The gunners needed time to man their guns. That time was over. The sky filled with streaks of tracer. Yellow, red, orange. Most of the *Flak* was not visible – only every eighth shell was a tracer. The invisible ones were more deadly. Ugly blobs of black smoke sprang from nothing as heavier shells exploded. There was little room for escape.

Ben reversed his course. Behind him was the black, rapidly rising pillar of smoke and a dirty piece of sky which had been the first jet. Ahead were many smaller, black smoke clouds with flaming centers. He dodged the ones he could while he searched for his wingman.

Ben looked back over his shoulder. Bob McCandliss' *Mustang* was covered with flames as yellow as its nose paint. "Get out, Mac, get out! Roll and bail. Roll and bail!" Ben yelled into his oxygen mask.

In his P-51, twenty-year-old Second Lieutenant Robert McCandliss twisted in his seat and stood up. He jumped. The wind wrapped a harness strap around his foot. Held him against the blazing fuselage. He was trapped. The airplane's nose fell toward the ground as it rolled onto its back.

2

DETROIT

1941

A cold rain was falling when Olive Drew walked out of the movie theater with her two sons. The bold, black headlines of the Detroit newspaper told her news no mother ever wants to hear.

To her teenage boys the headline was less frightening than a promise of excitement and adventure. One thing they could not do was let their mother see how pleased they were – as pleased as only youth can be. Keeping a serious expression was easy when they looked at their mother's face.

Urban was seventeen and a half. His brother Earl was about to turn sixteen. The day was December 7, 1941.

Olive Chasee Drew was a school teacher. Her years in the classroom made her well aware of how boys all across America were feeling this day. She especially knew what her own sons were thinking.

"Urban, this means it is time for you to go and fight for your country." She stood straight and touched his arm. "Whichever service you choose, do a good job of it. Make us all proud of you."

She turned on the wet sidewalk and put her other hand on Earl's shoulder. "Son, I pray the war doesn't last long enough for you to go too. But if it does, I know you will do well if you have to serve."

Arm in arm with her sons pulled close to her, Mrs. Olive Drew walked her family to their home on Hazelridge Avenue.

The war did last. Both her sons did join the United States Army Air Force. Both became fighter pilots. And she was as proud of the two stars displayed in her front window as of any of the medals her boys earned.

His mother may have been uncertain about which service he would join, but Urban Drew was not. To him there was only one. His tale is typical of so many boys who became men with wings.

Urban's favorite books were paperbacks with lurid drawings of *Spads* and *Fokkers* on the covers. He knew all the adventures of *G-8 and His Battle Aces*. He knew G-8's staunch wingmen were Nippy Weston and Bill Martin. He doodled airplanes in his school notebooks. He built both tissue covered, balsa-wood, flyable and carved pine models to play with.

Urban's first flight was a hop at the Detroit Airport his Uncle Pete bought for him. He did not notice the noise in the corrugated skin *Ford tri-motor*, because he spent the too few minutes with his nose pressed against the window.

A cousin took him up for twenty minutes in a *Taylorcraft* for his second flight. It was his last flight until he was an aviation cadet. That ride was better than the first; Urban Drew moved the control stick for the first time and made the little airplane go where he wanted it to go.

March twenty-first, 1942. My eighteenth birthday and I was first in line at the Army Air Corps recruiting center. The physical was easy. I'd been pretty athletic and was in good shape. The written test took awhile and I felt good about it, but they didn't tell you the results right away. I had to go home and sweat it out for several weeks. At last, the board sent a telegram and I went back to the recruiting center and was sworn in as a private in the U.S.Army. Then I had to go home and cool my heels again.

I remember thinking, "Don't those idiots know there's a war going on. I want to go now."

It was September before I was called up. Mother helped me pack. There wasn't much in the suitcase. We figured I wouldn't need any civilian clothes where I was going. Earl drove me to the station and I took a train to Chicago.

At the army collection center there, I was issued my first set of GI clothing. The top coat was at least eight sizes too big. Also got more needles stuck in me than a porcupine has quills. And we waited. At least, now I had company. Some corporal, who was acting awfully important for only two stripes on his sleeve, gathered us together and grandly announced that since there was going to be a wait for the train to Nashville the Army was, "Gonna' take you new soldier boys to a concert downtown."

The concert was conducted by Sigmund Romberg, the famous composer, and featured a knockout new girl singer he had discovered. It was a pretty good show. Afterwards, Mr. Romberg asked if there were any questions. One of the other recruits asked him how he picked a new singer. Romberg never hesitated and in that Hungarian accent of his, replied, "Sohn, I alvays know good voice ven I see vun." I never forgot that answer and used to quote it a lot.

I fell head over heels in love on the train ride.

Like all the trains I rode when I was in the Army – and I rode a lot – it pulled out after midnight. Why is it that Army trains have to leave at God-awful hours like that? There were a lot of guys in uniform on trains by then, so I spotted the girl right away. It was like a football scrimmage. I literally straight-armed a couple of guys, but I got the seat next to her.

Her name was Dallas and she was from Chicago. I'm sure we napped at some point, but it seemed we spent the whole night talking. We talked about where we were from, our families, our plans, our dreams. Several times our faces were real close and I could smell her lipstick.

To leave her side and step out into the bitter cold and snow on the railroad platform was a real shock. I never knew that Tennessee could get that cold!

Each barracks held forty men. One big room with twenty cots on each side. We were ordered to sleep as soon as we walked in and it seemed only minutes later a voice was bellowing, "Rise and shine, little soldier boys. Rise and shine." We struggled into our strange clothes, had a rushed shave and went outside for our first drill instruction. Left face. Right face. Attention. Parade rest. Hup, two, three, four. There in the dark and the cold and the snow, I remember thinking, "This is a hell of a way to become a fighter pilot."

I never saw Dallas again.

3

NASHVILLE

Cadet Days

Ben Drew's days as a cadet were a series of ups and downs. Fate decreed that his career could not be all good or all bad. Nor even mediocre. It would be highs and lows. He would no sooner do something well, then he would do something bad.

The beginning was misery typical of all cadet training. On the second day, after the early morning first drill, the cadets went to chow and were allowed back in their barracks. To a man, they flopped on their bunks. "Oh no you don't," the company sergeant yelled at them, "Bunks is for sleeping at night. Not in the day. This is day. Get one foot on the floor and keep it there. Or else. Unnerstand me?"

A chorus of "Yessir!" accompanied by the thumps of forty feet hitting the wooden floor answered him.

The next day, Private Urban Drew, serial 16082532, forgot. He was awakened from his nap by the thunder of an apoplectic sergeant an inch from his ear. He walked guard duty all that night carrying a field pack and rifle. The snow and cold had not gone away.

Two weeks into cadet training, Ben's grandmother died. Despite some sadness, he was glad to be away from the harassment of sergeants. He returned to Detroit on emergency leave.

Bad news came as a telegram advising Private Drew not to return to Nashville for two weeks. His class had been quarantined for an outbreak of measles.

I was crushed. There I was, ready to be the world's hottest pilot and they put me back two classes. It meant a two month delay. And to top it off, I was back with my old sergeant. And we weren't exactly buddies.

One early morning, he came storming in, screaming to get our asses in gear, we were moving to another barracks. I grumbled something about what was this man's army all about. Probably a little too loudly, because next thing I knew, a long, muscled arm had me by the neck and literally picked me out of my bed. Jammed me against the wall. I couldn't breathe or talk. The sergeant stuck his face into mine and asked, "What did you say, little soldier boy? I thought you said somethin'." I was choking to death. I couldn't speak. He looked at my bulging eyes and said, "Naw, can't hear nuthin'. I must have been mistaken." I was dropped like an empty sack. By the time I caught my breath, I couldn't pack fast enough and moved out with my buddies.

The next step in training was pre-flight at Maxwell Army Air Base. Ben and his class were loaded aboard a train at midnight and left for Montgomery, Alabama.

Pre-flight was a step up from Nashville. They were now Cadets instead of recruits. Their immediate supervisors were senior cadets. Not that daily life was any easier. Classroom subjects were related to flying and that kept each man's goal in sight, but the West Point system of hazing was in full effect. Cadets marched everywhere. When an officer, even a cadet officer, spoke to them – they never spoke to the officer, only answered – they were in a *brace* – rigidly straight back, arms clamped to sides, elbows back, chest out, chin tucked in so hard they could not talk if they were allowed to. They walked endless *tours* for minor infractions. A full night's sleep became a rarity. Quarters bounced on tautly made beds. Shoes and boots were always spit-shiny, mirror-bright. From the first day, the upperclassmen rode the new cadets. "Nothing personal. We went through it. Now it's your turn. Only one out of ten of you will make it through. Remember, one out of ten."

Marching is considered the most basic of military skills. As much as all recruits hate the time spent walking endlessly in geometric patterns going nowhere, marching has its advantages. Number one, marching is still the best way to get a group of men, intact, from one place to another. Number two, it teaches teamwork. Each individual subordinates what he wants to do, to what the group must do... together. In addition to physical skills, marching requires concentration, and despite the appearance of automatons, each man has to think. To be aware of what is happening, of where he is, where the formation is, what will, might, happen next. For pilots, many of the reactions taught in hours of marching drill are used in flying formation.

As an athlete who played team sports and young man with a instinctive feel for leadership, Ben was good at drill. He could never admit it to his cadet classmates, but he actually enjoyed marching. He found himself encouraging and coaching the others.

Midway through their time at Maxwell, a parade for a visiting British general was announced. A chance to show-off, to look good.

There is marching and there is Marching. The basic half dozen commands can be combined to make patterns. They can be repeated rapidly, one following the other, to create a rhythm which transcends mere walking in step.

The first words of a marching command are what to do. Then the final word is "barked", giving the exact instant to do it. For every command there is a specific instant – usually as the left foot hits the ground. When not giving commands, the leader will normally count cadence to keep all the men in step. A simple, "left, right, left," or "Hut, two, three, four." are usual. "Hut", replaces "one" because it is sharper and more exact. Sharpness in drill is a matter of micro-seconds.

Cadet Drew excelled at close order drill. He was a natural at calling the difficult cadences. The parade for the general was such an impressive performance that he was made a cadet officer. For parades, he was entitled to wear the swooping, peaked stripes of West Point, a shiny, brown leather Sam Browne belt and carry a saber in a silver scabbard.

4

TUSCALOOSA

Flying at last

My first flights were a disaster. Well, the flying itself must have been OK, but my instructor was a problem. I mean my flying career almost ended before it started. I don't think he was a particularly good instructor anyway, but the bigger problem was I couldn't understand the man.

I grew up in Detroit. Lots of my friends were sons of immigrants; Germans, Poles. And I'd hear some pretty thick accents from the other side of the river. Heck, my grandmother was Canadien, *I mean as French Canadian as can be. She lived with us and I always spoke French when I was with her. Learned years later it was a rather unique form of French, but it was another language. My ear was attuned to different speech. But this guy...*

You're nervous enough meeting your first instructor – any instructor – I never was able to relax with another pilot in the same plane for years after I got my wings. Your fate is in his hands. All your hopes and dreams could go on his whim. Nowadays, we call it "personality conflict". At the time, the air force could have cared less; there were simply too many kids who wanted to fly.

He was dark skinned and dark haired and wore a thin, black mustache; like "Smiling Jack", the heroic pilot of the comics. Only he didn't look heroic. He reminded me of a short, pudgy Cesar Romero. In the rush to set up a program to train thousands of pilots, the air force had taken anyone who even vaguely knew how to teach flying. Oh, I'm sure there were some good instructors. But he wasn't one of them. His accent was the obvious problem; only later did I realize he would not have been a good teacher in the air even if his English was flawless. He came from Cuba. Apparently, not that long ago.

There was no intercom in the Stearman; just the Gosport tube with its one way conversation. Pick up a garden hose and put one end in your ear while someone talks into the other end. That's what the Gosport sounded like; all hollow and echo-ey. And that's without wind noise and the racket from the engine. Once in the air, I don't think I understood a word he said—I only got about half of them on the ground. I don't think he was comfortable in the air. He would talk faster and louder. His accent got worse. And any patience he may have had, disappeared.

Fortunately, learning to fly is a lot of imitation. He'd do a maneuver. I'd follow on the controls and then do it myself. Any suggestions or corrections the Cuban had were lost coming through the Gosport. He was frustrated, and so was I.

When he was really wound up, he'd unstrap – lap belt and shoulder straps – heave himself around with his knees on the seat, lean on the turtle-deck between the cockpits and scream at me.

Once I figured out that I couldn't understand him anyway, the hardest part was keeping a straight face. "I could get rid of this little bastard right now," I'd think. "Just pop the stick forward. A quick little push and whoosh, out he'd go. Just like that. Up, up and away. Whoosh. Claim I'd hit an air pocket or something. Had to be a rule against unstrapping in flight. His own damn fault. Push forward. Whoosh, and away."

I never did. I would do anything to stay in the program.

After a week of misery, he screamed that I'd never be a pilot and recommended I be dropped from training. I was destroyed.

The next day found Urban standing in a rigid brace in front of the desk of an army lieutenant as he sounded off with, "Aviation Cadet Urban L. Drew, 16082532, reporting as ordered, Sir!"

The majority of the instructors at a primary training base were civilians, part of the CPT, Civil Pilot Training program. However, there was always a cadre of regular army aviators to give check rides and make the final decision on whether a student could become a military pilot.

The Lieutenant looked up from the pile of paper on his desk. "Drew, your instructor does not think you can hack the program. What's your side of the story?"

Urban explained the problems he had with understanding the heavily accented speech. "I think I am a pretty good flyer, Sir."

The Lieutenant smiled at the cocksure statement. "I'll fly with you myself. Be on the flight line at 0600 tomorrow. We'll see if you're half the hotshot you think you are."

Throughout the flight, Urban Drew worried because the Lieutenant said so little. Only terse requests for maneuvers came through the *Gosport*. "Give me a two turn spin.", "Do a figure-eight around that tree and the farm house over there." Sometimes not even a voice, but a hand waved to show a direction or altitude change. "Back to the field." Urban flew two touch-and-goes. "Stop after the next one."

Here it comes, thought Urban, the end of the world. Please, please, God, I want to fly.

When the *Stearman* was chocked and the prop stopped turning, the Lieutenant immediately climbed out. Stepping off the wing, he said only, "Meet me inside," as he passed the rear cockpit.

Urban's thoughts dragged his shoulders down more than the weight of the parachute did. His walk to the hangar was long and slow. Urban slung his parachute on the counter in the equipment room. He hoped not for the last time.

The meeting was brief.

"Drew, you did well." The army pilot smiled as he spoke. "I'll take over as your instructor. You're going to be a fine pilot. 0800 tomorrow. Dismissed."

Urban floated back to the cadet barracks. All the weight was gone. He could not wait to tell his buddies. With the cruelty of young men subject to the same consequences, they had been riding him about how it was all over, washout time, off to the walking army. The flight he had just had was called a "Maytag" after a popular make of clothes washer; only he hadn't washed out.

The Lieutenant was quiet again on the next flight and, unlike the previous day, they did not leave the traffic pattern at the field, but practiced landings. After the fourth, his instructor told Urban, "Pull over on to the grass."

Odd, thought Urban, I've always gone to the ramp before.

His instructor climbed from the front cockpit, parachute bumping awkwardly. He stopped on the black walk-stripe on the bi-plane's wing. "Do two touch and goes. Then stop and pick me up." He patted Urban's shoulder. "Good luck." He walked off to the side, slipped out of the parachute straps and hunkered in the deep, green grass to watch.

I couldn't believe it. The moment I'd been waiting for. I was going to fly an airplane... alone! Two days before I thought my flying was all over. Gone. Finis. Now I was going solo. I had six hours, eighteen minutes in the air. If it wasn't the record for low time at Tuscaloosa, it was a contender. Ten, twelve hours was considered normal before solo. I had a little more than six. And, despite my earlier problems, I felt ready.

What can I say about my first solo that hasn't been said before? I had all the typical feelings. Remember them all vividly. Accomplishment. Pride. The mechanical facts too. How much better the airplane climbed with only me on board. The view forward with no one else's head and shoulders in the way. The landings were good, not perfect, but good. I critiqued each one to myself. Mostly I remember the sheer joy of flying. The Stearman PT-19 was, in reality, cumbersome, something of a dog to fly, but on that glorious day, she was smooth and responsive, responding to my gentlest urgings. By the time I taxied onto the grass to pick up the Lieutenant I was on top of the world. I was the ace of the base. I could do no wrong. My grin must have been splitting my swollen head in two. The grin and the feeling lasted the rest of the day, all that evening in barracks gloating over my classmates, all the next morning at early breakfast and about fifteen minutes into my next flight. What is the expression about pride and the fall?

5

MISSISSIPPI

The Potato Patch

The next day began simply enough. The lieutenant told me to takeoff at 0800 hours and fly to Auxiliary Field Three. There were four or five fields like this nearby where students would practice. He would be there early with another cadet who would fly back solo while the Lieutenant and I flew back dual. I had been to Aux Three before and wasn't worried about getting there on my own. I wasn't worried about anything that morning; about anything at all. I still felt like the Ace-of-the-base. Solo with less hours than any cadet had ever done! Wow!

I got a green light from the control shack and off I went. I carefully flew the proper departure pattern and headed for Aux Three. Along the way, I'd bank or dip the nose out of the shear joy of feeling the airplane move. And every time my eyes swept forward, I'd admire the emptiness of the front cockpit.

After fifteen minutes of skylarking along, it occurred to me that I should have been over the auxiliary field by now. I guess I really didn't know how to get there. With my Cuban screaming at me the other time I was there, I hadn't paid much attention to where I was.

I did some big turns to the right and left, looking around for some landmark. I turned in a full circle. Nothing was familiar. I had no idea where I was.

Airmail pilots in their Jennies *and* DeHavillands *used to find a railroad track and follow it to a town. Drop down and read the name of the town on the station or nearby water tower. I learned that in one of the pulp flying books I read as a kid. I would try it. I picked a direction and flew along over the unfamiliar countryside of rural Alabama.*

A pilot cannot ignore the fuel gage in a Stearman. *It is right in front of his nose. The gage is a glass tube that sticks down from the bottom of the upper wing. Whenever you look forward, there it is. Inside the tube is a thin rod with a disk on the end. The upper end of the rod has a big cork on it. The cork floats on top of the gasoline in the tank inside the wing. The rod, and the tube, are as long as the tank is deep. Nothing electric. No fancy gears and levers. When the disk is on the bottom of the tube, the gas is gone. My disk that morning was lower than I had ever seen it... and it was getting lower.*

At last I found a railroad track across a large plowed field, in front of a row of trees. Those two shiny strips of silver looked awfully good. I put the Stearman *into a steep bank and turned hard to follow the tracks. I couldn't lose them now.*

Fields, some green, some still red earth, passed by. I flew over stands of trees, Pines mostly. There were buildings, farmhouses, barns, shacks. I flew on. Hoping for a town and station. My prayers increased with each time that little disk bumped the bottom of the tube as the fuel sloshed.

Ahead. A town. Buildings. And a fat cylinder of a water tower. I fly lower. Don't care if I get in trouble for flat-hatting. I want to be low and close enough to see the brush strokes on that town's name. The tower comes closer. It's painted silver. Big black letters. Easy to read. D-A-N-C-Y. Dancy? I have no idea. None. Who am I trying to kid? I'm from Detroit. Up north. Until the army, never more than a hundred miles from home.

The space between the disk and the bottom of the tube is down to a fraction of an inch. I do not have many choices left.

I will land in a farm field. It will mean the walking army for certain, but better that than crash and be dead. Yesterday – heck, this morning – I was Ace-of-the-base; now this.

Rules I had been taught pop into my head. It is better to land while the engine is running than run completely out of fuel. Land into the wind... when possible. In a plowed field, land with the furrows. Going into trees, aim between two trunks – the wings coming off will absorb energy. Tighten your straps. TIGHTEN your straps. If my straps were any tighter, I would get gangrene. I chose a farm field, freshly plowed – the tractor was plowing fresh furrows on the far side – they were lined up close to where I thought the wind was from. I flew downwind higher than normal in case the engine did quit. Turned on final and slipped her down just as pretty as can be.

Then I saw the power lines.

Right in front of me. Big, black wires stretched between two poles I hadn't noticed. Smack on my nose. Too close to try and go around. I instinctively pulled the stick back into my gut. Airspeed was already low. The airplane shuddered as 2,700 pounds of machinery stalled, stopped flying and fell into the dirt.

The Stearman folks in Wichita built a helluva tough bird. The softness of the field helped. And the big, fat tires. And the stiff oleo struts. And God.

I didn't roll very far. Don't remember touching the brakes either. Never came close to the trees at the end. Switched off the mags and cut the fuel at some point. Don't remember that either. It was very quiet.

A regular chuf-chuf-chuf noise came from the tractor. It was a one cylinder John Deere job. I figured the farmer would be over any minute and took my time getting out of the cockpit. First thing I did was walk around the all yellow airplane. Just like I was doing a pre-flight inspection. I couldn't believe it, so I went around again looking more closely. There was nothing wrong. Not one thing was broken. The farmer was still chuf-chuffing along.

I waved my arm once when I thought he was looking my way. Nothing. So I walked across the lumpy soil to where he was plowing. He stopped when he got next to me. The engine making slow popping noises as it idled.
"Hello," I said. "Where am I?"

"Whaddya mean, where are ya?" He had on a torn straw hat and collarless, long sleeve shirt. "Ain'cha from thet army base, prac'sin landin's?"

"Sir, I wouldn't be doing landings and takeoffs in your potato patch for practice. I'm from Tuscaloosa and seem to have run out of gas."

The farmer pushed his hat back on his head. "Well son, you's in the state of Mississippi now."

Mississippi! My heart fell, bottomed out in my shoes. I was a whole state away from where I was supposed to be. This was it. Washout. No wings for Mrs. Drew's boy.

The farmer did have a telephone and I called the base at Tuscaloosa. Of course, by then I was overdue. And to add to my problems one of the flight instructors answered the phone. The obnoxious one that all us cadets disliked.

"Drew, where the hell are you?"

"I'm at this farmhouse, Sir. The farmer tells me I'm in the state of Mississippi."

"Holy shit! How did you wind up in Mississippi? Of all the stupid cadets... How bad's the airplane? What's broken on it?"

"The airplane's fine, Sir. Absolutely OK." He never did ask how I was.

"Well, keep your dumb ass there. I'll bring a couple of mechanics and a jeep. Cadet, put the farmer on."

After giving directions, the farmer went and plowed the last rows on that field, came back and made some coffee, which we were drinking when the three men arrived in a Jeep. I don't remember what the Mississippi farmer and I talked about while we waited; I was numb. My life was over.

At the potato patch, the instructor gazed at the airplane and sized up the field. "Well, if a dumb ass like you can get it in, I can get it out. You men, push it down to the end. In front of the trees."

Ben and the two sergeants picked up the *Stearman's* tail and pulled it backwards to the tree line that Ben had been so worried about running into. They put gas in the tank and rechecked the airplane. The civilian flight instructor strapped in and the sergeants helped get the engine started. Since they had arrived, the sergeants had said nothing besides "Yessir" and "Nossir".

Ben called up to the cockpit, "Do you want me to get in, Sir?"

"Nooo. You ride back with the men. I'll do this all by myself." The sergeants were already heading for the far end of the field near the dirt road. Ben hurried to catch up. It was not a long walk.

As he came alongside, one sergeant said to Ben, "Cadet, you know he ain't gonna make it. Field's too short." He did not seem overly concerned. Off to the side was a wagon loaded with a foot deep layer of manure. They stopped near it and turned to watch.

The sound of a *Pratt and Whitney* engine at full power came from across the patch. The tail came up too soon and the airplane swerved and jumped across a furrow. The jump made it swerve more and it bounced and swerved across more furrows. The plane bounced and jumped until it was heading diagonally across the field.

"Hit the deck!", one of the sergeants yelled. "Hit the deck." Ben needed no urging and the three of them dove beneath the wagon.

The airplane missed crashing into the center of the wagon which would have killed them all. Instead, the lower left wing smashed into the solid, heavy wagon and tore off, slewing the *Stearman* up and around. The propeller and engine broke off as the fuselage lifted in the air and fell on its back. The impact tore off both right wings.

Motion stopped. Noise stopped. Falling chunks of dirt, manure and airplane stopped. No one moved. The three men lay in the dirt, hands over their heads. When he heard the sergeants look around, Ben lifted his head. The wrecked *Stearman* lay on its back. The crumpled tail, the one remaining wing and what was left of the nose held the cockpit opening off the ground. The pilot hung upside down in his straps. The top of his head two inches from the reddish dirt. He was not moving.

The men stood slowly, looking for dripping fluid – fuel or blood. Cautiously they went nearer the wreck; ready to run or hit the dirt if it exploded or burned.

Nothing dripped. Nothing burned.

Ben went closer. He dropped on his hands and knees. The front of the khaki uniform he flew in was already covered with dirt. More would not make any difference. He bent his head down close to the pilot hanging upside-down. "Sir? Sir, can you hear me?"

The instructor's eyes popped open. His face swung towards Ben. Their noses were inches apart. He began a stream of invective that began foully soft, grew in volume and scatology until it was a stream of abuse and filth condemning all cadets, sergeants, farmers, their fields, airplanes, and the world in general. Spit flew from his upside down mouth and a ridiculous trickle of drool went "up" his cheeks. The swearing ended with a loud, "Get me out of here!" They were the last words Ben ever heard from the man.

The sergeants and Ben tugged the much reduced fuselage structure high enough for the errant pilot to wiggle out. He stalked straight to the Jeep. The farmer was back on his one cylinder tractor, chuff-chuffing away from them. Ben and the sergeants looked around, saw the wreckage was not a hazard, was clear of the plowed ground and could wait. They looked at each other. Shrugged. Got into the Jeep for the long, uncomfortable... and very quiet ride back to Tuscaloosa.

It was all over. All over. I only thought it was over with the Cuban. This time it had to be all over. And my buddies, my roommates, were no damn help at all. "Hey Urban, only two things happen to schmoes who wreck one of Uncle Sam's airplanes," they'd say, "two things. You go to the walking army. Oorrr..." The bastards would really draw it out. "*...they throw you in Fort Leavenworth where you make little rocks out of big ones.*"

They were only teasing. Riding me the way we all did to each other. It was typical of teenagers in a competitive program. Hey, I knew I hadn't crashed the airplane. I'd saved it. They knew that too. But the ribbing hurt. I was worried. More than I'd ever been. I may not have crashed it, but I was the one who got lost. Got lost by being dumb. Got lost by dreaming about the day before instead of thinking about the minute ahead. It was a miserable two days.

On the third day, I was instructed to report to the Commandant of Cadets. His name was Captain Noel Cumbaa and he was quite a gentleman. He was from the area and had graduated from the University of Alabama right there in Tuscaloosa. He had a reputation as a nice guy. I certainly hoped it was so. My future was in his hands.

I spent hours getting ready. My trouser creases were never sharper. My shoes never shinier. I had rehearsed what I thought I was going to say, over and over.

I rapped three times on the wooden door and, after hearing a sharp, "Come in," marched to three paces in front of his desk, hit the brace position and, as clearly as I could with my chin against my chest, said, "Cadet Urban L. Drew reporting as ordered, Sir."

Captain Cumbaa looked up from what I assumed was a folder containing all my crimes and misdeeds, waved his hand at a chair, and said, "Please sit down."

Please?

"Ah used an inspection of the crash site as an excuse to use a little guvmint gas to take my wife for a drive t'other evenin'." His tone was as soft as his accent. "Ah paced off that farmer's field. Both ways."

He had been sitting straight and now leaned forward. "You, Cadet Drew, do not have the expertise to land an airplane in that field. It is too short. Far too short. Tell me, how in the name of all that's holy, did you do it."

"Well Sir," I replied. "I guess I was lucky." And I told him about seeing the wires at the last minute and snatching the stick back in my lap and how the airplane must have stalled because it came down with a helluva thump, but it must have hit on all three wheels and the fat main tires and the newly plowed dirt absorbed the shock because nothing broke and the roll was short, really short, and there I was."

"Ah guess that luck is the word. What you did was exactly what was needed to get into a field that small. But you couldn't have known that. Luck it most certainly was." Captain Cumbaa leaned back in his chair again. "You know that that damn fool of an instructor was kicked out of here. His draft board will have him in the walkin' army in nuthin' flat."

He leaned forward again, leaning his arms on the desk. "'Course there's the matter of you gettin' more'n a little lost." I sagged in the chair. I had started to think I'd get off OK. "Tell you what, Cadet Drew. You go back to your quarters and write out for me, 100 times, 'I will never get lost again.'"

I jumped to my feet and saluted. "Yessir. I'll do that. Right away. Yessir. Thank you, Sir." I did an about-face and left the office before he could change his mind or add anything more.

I became a fanatic about navigation. I gave ground school classes in it special attention, asked for extra problems. Read maps like the other cadets read comic books. Added knowing exactly where I was to all the other items to do on every flight. Was constantly working out the course to home base, to outlying bases. I made navigating second nature. Once, when I forgot, it lead to my greatest screw-up. Yet, another time, my navigating skills were responsible for my best achievement.

But on that day, it was enough that I was still in the program. That my punishment had been a school boy's. Back in the barracks, the others all asked if I was washed out. "Hell no," I replied. "Not only am I not washed out, I'm a hero. A hero."

6

MALDEN, MO

In Trouble Again

Francis Xavier Dunnigan was the son of a Boston bar owner. He drank more than anyone I ever knew – and in the Army Air Forces during wartime, that was saying a lot. Me? I never even had a drink until I was instructing at Bartow. Mother simply did not allow it. Alcohol, swearing and loose women. All on the sin list while I was growing up. That changed in a hurry during the war.

Francis Xavier kept six bottles of Bourbon under his bed at all times. He was fond of taking a snort, or two, whenever the spirit moved him. Which was frequently. How he managed to stay out of trouble and get his wings was a minor mystery to all of us who knew him. But get his wings, he did.

Francis Xavier Dunnigan was killed flying a B-25 Mitchell *bomber in the Southwest Pacific. For his bravery in attacking Japanese ships that day, he was awarded the Distinguished Service Cross... posthumously. A bottle of bourbon may even have been tucked under his pilot's seat that day. It does not matter; he was a superb pilot and a brave man.*

Xavier was one of my four roommates in basic training. We still lived in a barracks, but it was only four to a room and we had more space, including our own study desks. That's how I knew about his secret booze cache. Besides flying, there wasn't much to do at Malden. The town a few *miles down the road was off-limits to cadets; supposedly, because of a high VD rate. After the delectable young southern belles the University of Alabama supplied back in Tuscaloosa, restriction to the base was a severe shock. Time was heavy on our hands, so naturally there was a lot of boozing .*

Malden was a basic flight training base, the fourth stage on a cadet's path to pilot wings. First had been basic recruit training. We called it pre-pre-flight. Then pre-flight proper when we finally worked at something to do with flying. Next came primary, basic, and advanced flight training. So far for me this had been in Nashville, Maxwell, Tuscaloosa and, now, Malden.

The airplane we flew at Malden was the Vultee BT-13. *It seemed modern and sleek compared to the* Stearman. *It was a monoplane and all metal. The landing gear were fixed in place, but it did have a canopy that fully enclosed both cockpits. And it had a radio and an intercom system which meant no more of the despised* Gosport *tubes. We could actually converse with our instructor in the other seat. As students, we started in the front seat unlike what we had done in the* Stearman. *From there we learned how to fly the BT-13 and honed our basic flight skills. About the time we were feeling comfortable, we found ourselves in the back seat... with a bag over our head, learning to fly instruments. Although the canvas cover pulled up and over to obscure the view of any and all outside references, it was not really a bag, but more like a tent. It was called "the Bag" because inside it was dark, claustrophobic and tended to restrict your thinking as much as it did your vision. Because the Pratt and Whitney 450 horsepower engine tended to shake the whole airplane all the time, the airplane was usually called the "Vultee Vibrator".*

One fine Saturday afternoon, Francis Xavier had a great idea. Actually, it was a very stupid idea, but I was so bored hanging around the base doing nothing that I went along with it.

A flight maneuver we were practicing a lot at the time was the pylon eight. It is a ground reference maneuver which calls for a fair amount of pilot skill. It is still part of the check ride for commercial pilots. Basically, the maneuver consists of making a turn around two points on the ground making a figure eight when seen from above. By varying altitude and hence airspeed and varying angle of bank any effect of the wind could be canceled and a perfect eight pattern flown. None of the instruments were of any help which is why it was called a ground reference maneuver.

"Urban," said Francis Xavier, "let us go and practice pylon eights on the lawn in front of the commandant's office." His speech was perfect, but the boozy smell of his breath told me the spirit had moved him to have some spirit. "It's Saturday and I know the commandant won't be in his office. The mechanics left an airplane tug behind our barracks. We can practice with that."

What the heck, I thought. There's no harm in that. Sounds like fun. Sure nothing else to do around here. To this day, I don't really know why I went along with him. Boredom. It had to have been pure boredom.

Getting the Jeep-like tug started was not a problem. Like all military vehicles it either did not use a key or the key was left in the ignition. On a sleepy weekend afternoon, no one noticed them on the street. Francis Xavier drove. Urban stood, hung on to the seat back and gave advice. The lawn in front of the commandant's office was wide and smooth, and not made to withstand an airplane tug being driven in tight circles at high speed. The tires tore up swatches of turf.

The two cadets had completed three pylon eights and as they came around to start their fourth, found themselves looking at the Commandant of Cadets standing on the porch, leaning against a post. Francis Xavier slammed on the brakes.

"Are you two having fun?" The commandant was calm, his tone conversational. "Not very good for the lawn 'though, is it?" The army captain was so calm, the pair began to relax. "Why don't you come over here so we can talk?" The commandant walked down the steps and two yards onto his ruined grass. The cadets got off the tug and walked to meet him. When they were three feet away, the captain's smile vanished. "Cadet Dunnigan. Cadet Drew." His voice was calm with their names, but each word after was louder in a crescendo of controlled rage. With every phrase his face grew redder. With every minute their crime became more drastic. The commandant's tirade lasted ten minutes. Dunnigan and Drew stayed in a rigid brace for those ten, eternally long, minutes, scarcely breathing, never moving their eyes from absolutely straight ahead. It was a chewing-out to end all chewing-outs. Drill-master sergeants of long experience would have been proud.

Perhaps because he thought the dressing down was effective; perhaps because he had been amused by the tractor spinning across the grass; perhaps because he was anticipating the rest of the weekend at home; for whatever reason, the commandant took no drastic action against the errant pair. They did get an entry in their official records. They did have the cost of repairing the sod taken out of their already meager pay. And they did walk "tours" every night. For the remaining five weeks in Basic Flight training, Cadets Drew and Dunnigan spent the day flying and in class, then from 7 to 11 PM they would march around and around the perimeter of the airbase carrying a rifle and wearing a sixty pound field pack.

Unfortunately for Urban Drew's nerves, he was also involved in a taxi accident at this time. All the BT-13's were parked in a long row and it was hard to see who was pulling out when taxiing between the rows. Another cadet chewed up the tail of Urban's "Vibrator" with his prop as he pulled out. There he was, walking tours for one misdemeanor and sweating out another possible wash-out event. It was two long days before a board determined that the other cadet was one hundred percent at fault. Drew was admonished "To be more careful while taxiing."

Cadets Drew and Dunnigan were not thrown out of the program. They easily could have been.

7

MARIANNA

...who you know.

There are times when it is not what you know as who you know.

There was never a question in Ben's mind as to what type of pilot he wanted to be. He wanted to fly fighters. He had since reading flying stories in grammar school. Toward the end of Basic in Malden, cadets were asked their preferences. Ben wrote FIGHTERS in capital letters in all five blanks.

He got what he wanted. He was assigned to advanced training in single engine AT-6 aircraft. Training that would lead to assignment to fighters.

The train to Marianna, Florida left at midnight. The ride lasted the rest of the night and most of the next day. The train stopped at every town.

When the cadets checked in at the air force base, there was a surprise for Ben. He was told to report to the Commandant of Cadets living quarters.

Surprised and puzzled, Ben walked to the officers' housing area and knocked on the door to one of a row of identical, small, wood framed, white houses differentiated only by the letter L painted on a square sign screwed over the front door. The Commandant of Cadets at Marianna was Major Leslie Seppala. The name sounded familiar to Ben as they shook hands. The mystery was solved when Mrs Seppala come out of the kitchen. She had taught Ben at Wayne University during the one semester he had at college before enlisting.

Major Seppala explained that when he was going over the records of the incoming class, he noticed Wayne State and asked his wife about Ben Drew. She had favorable memories of the freshman in her English class. He also wanted to know about the incident at Malden. Ben's explanation must have been a good one because Major Seppala and his wife laughed about the pylon-eights in a tug.

"Well, Urban," the major said, "you were a cadet commander in preflight and again in primary. For obvious reasons, you weren't in advanced." He shook his head at the thought of his lawn. "I need a good man to be commander here. I am appointing you senior cadet commander for class 43-I. Don't disappoint me… and no more driving tugs around."

Ben had his Sam Browne belt, saber and stripes back. When graduation day came he marched at the front of the class for the final parade.

8

LEIPHEIM

First Flight

The *Messerschmitt 263* looks like a giant frog. A giant winged frog. The ribs of the clamshell doors at the nose protrude like a frog's bones. The doors open left and right like a twisted frog's mouth. The small cockpit windows atop the droopy roundness of the nose are eyes. The tail is as slim as a polliwog's. The *Me 263* squats flat on the ground. The green wings of the 180 foot wide hulk are 29 feet above the ground. It does not look like it can fly.

It cannot.

At least, not by itself. The *Me263* was a glider. The largest ever built. The Germans named it *der Gigant*, the Giant. It took an enormous effort to get the *Gigant* into the air. Two three engined *Ju52s* were used. And a trio of twin-engined *Me110* fighters called a *Troika-Schlepp* was tried. Later, two Heinkel bombers were fused at the wing and a fifth engine installed at the joint for a tow aircraft. Hazardous and unstable liquid fuel rockets were fastened under the huge wings to assist take off.

The *Me263* was designed to carry enormous loads. A *PzKpfW IV* tank weighing 22 tonnes could go through the frog mouth. 200 fully equipped troops in a special double decker arrangement could be carried aloft. Indeed, until jumbo jet crashes in the '70's, the worst aviation disaster occurred when the rockets on one wing of a *Me263* did not ignite. The giant airplane swerved and fouled the cables of all three *Troika-Schlepp Me110* tow aircraft. There was a load of soldiers onboard when all four airplanes crashed. There were no survivors. The accident did not slow the program. The heavy lift capability was needed too much.

On July 18, 1942 the center of attention at Leipheim Airfield was a much smaller airplane which also did not have propellers. Sitting cockily on the concrete ramp was the third prototype of the *Messerschmitt 262*. The *262* looked all the sleeker for the *Gigants* scattered about. So much was radical in the design that the engineers were reluctant to make too much too new. For that reason, the *Me262* had a conventional tailwheel. This meant the long streamlined nose and the jet intakes pointed toward the sky while the tail surfaces were close to the ground. This airplane looked like it wanted to fly.

The *Me262* was 35 feet from nose to tail and the swept back wings reached 41 feet from tip to tip. Small compared to the *Gigants* standing nearby like stone monoliths.

The first prototype, the *Me 262 V1*,(the V stood for *versuchsmuster;* experimental in German), had flown in April, but it had been an awkward experience. The jet engines were behind schedule, so the Messerschmitt factory installed a conventional piston engine of 750 horsepower driving a two bladed propeller in the nose. The test pilots reported no problems with the airframe over the course of several flights. *BMW 003* engines were fitted to the first prototype, but they both failed soon after lift-off and the airplane was damaged in the forced landing. The *V1* proved the *Me262* airframe could fly with conventional power. The *V2* remained on the factory floor for ground tests. A different type of engine was fortunately available and was installed on prototype number three. The engine was the Junkers built *Jumo 004*. It was an axial-flow turbojet of sophisticated design and would power all subsequent *Me262s*. The early *Jumo 004* produced 1,323 pounds of thrust and would drive the airplane to speeds unanticipated by the designers. The *V3* was about to see if the swept wing airplane could fly jet propelled.

An unsuspected problem had come up during high speed taxi tests on the *V3*. At what should have been take off speed, the elevator had no effect on the airplane's pitch. During flights of the *V1* the propeller provided plenty of airflow over the elevator, but with the jets out on the wings, the low sitting tail was blanked off by the fuselage and wings. The ingenious solution was simple. Simple and risky. At high speed, tap the wheel brakes to get the nose down, the tail up into the airstream. Too much tap and airspeed would be lost. A fraction more than that and the nose would slam into the ground.

Flugkapitain Fritz Wendel was to be the pilot. A long time Messerschmitt test pilot, he had flown the *Me262V1* and done the taxi tests on the *V3*. He had proved that a quick little squeeze on the brakes worked.

Ten mechanics were gathered around the *Me262* to get it ready for flight. They fussed over it like a mother sending her child to the first day of school. When they declared it ready, Wendel strapped into the cockpit. The "blackmen" continued to fuss near the nacelles and over Wendel's shoulder as he started the *Jumo* engines. A *Gigant* hulked at the edge of the concrete ramp.

Wendel taxied the V3 out rapidly, bouncing over the grass to the end of the paved runway. He lined up and carefully pushed the twin throttles up. The 262 started to roll, faster and faster. A road crossed the center of the runway. The blast of dust and dirt was hardly noticed as the tail abruptly lifted and the slim nose came down. Wendel had again timed it perfectly,. The jet sat flat. It accelerated, balanced on its main wheels. Rotation was not noticeable – the airplane simply rose off the ground.

The flight was not long. Wendel felt out the differences jet power made to the 262 airframe. He did make one pass over the runway, rather high, to show off for the mechanics, engineers and officials.

His approach to landing was low and flat. After touchdown, as the 262 slowed and put its tail down, a burst of smoke billowed from the left engine. Flames were visible at the tailpipe. Wendel braked to a stop, flipped the canopy open and climbed out in a hurry. Fire trucks and men ran out to the airplane. A leak had puddled fuel in the tailpipe. When the tail settled, the hot exhaust ignited the fuel. The fire wasn't serious; the *Me262V3* flew again that afternoon.

A landmark in aviation had been achieved. Other jet powered aircraft had flown by then, but this was the first flight of a jet powered, combat fighter. The airplane was a world beater. Nothing then in existence could fly as fast, fly as high. It was capable of dominating the skies over Europe. It would take more years to develop, and its full potential would never be realized, but by the end of 1944, it was the world's most formidable aircraft.

9

BARTOW

No Navigation

Ben did exceedingly well in fighter training at Bartow, Florida. And then wished he had not.

Training at Bartow was in the P-51 *Mustang*. The airplane that was called the best fighter of World War II. The 54th Fighter Group had been one of the first groups to enter combat when the war started. It had flown Curtis P-40s in the bitter Aleutian campaign. In 1943, the 54th Group had be converted to a Replacement Training Unit, RTU, and assigned *Mustangs*. Colonel Ward Harker was the commanding officer and he had with him many veterans who had fought the Japanese in the Pacific and a select group of pilots who had flown against the *Luftwaffe* in North Africa and Sicily. At the time Ben reported in, the 54th group probably had a higher concentration of combat veterans than any RTU in the United States.

They flew early models of the *Mustang* at Bartow. By some quirk, the second model was designated the P-51A, so the pilots referred to the first version as the "P-51 period". In addition, the RTU used A-36's, the ground attack version of the *Mustang* with dive brakes and four, long 20 millimeter cannons sticking out of the wing. The A-36's were as seasoned as the pilots who flew them, having been shipped back from Africa. The P-51 "periods", A's and A-36's all used the *Allison V-12* engine. Allison engined *Mustang*s were great airplanes at low altitude. Above 12,000 feet their performance dropped off which made them unsuitable for first line combat, but still good enough for training.

It was the British who put the Rolls-Royce *Merlin* engine with a two stage, two speed supercharger into the *Mustang* and made a high altitude fighter out of it. The American Packard motor company built thousands of *Merlins* under license. The P-51B had a *Merlin* engine and some of them began to arrive in the RTU in 1944.

There was none of this two seat trainer version of everything back then. My first flight in the P-40 back before I had my wings was absolutely alone, a real solo. That's why they gave us those ten hours. See if we had the confidence to strap on a high powered machine and get it in the air. The bomber and transport guys didn't have to do that.

My first time in the Mustang *was that way too. We went over the airplane in a class room for a couple of days. Then an instructor hunkered on the wing or put his butt on the cockpit rail while he went over the switches and procedures. In the meanwhile, you spent as much time in the cockpit as you could because the last check before flying was a to find every switch, knob and lever blindfolded.*

I won't say it was an instant romance. The first flight left me gasping and very, very impressed with her power and speed, but it sure didn't take long until I was head over heels in love with that airplane. After about five hours I was happily buzzing the Okefenokee and Okechobee Swamps; doing barrel rolls at tree top height. She was so responsive and powerful. I could hardly wait to get overseas and try her out.

Bartow changed a lot in Drew's life, including his name. Military pilots have some innate tendency to nicknames. It wasn't long before Urban became Ben. The name stayed with him from then on.

When his class was about due to graduate, Ben Drew could not wait to get his posting. He was standing by the bulletin board when the assignment list was thumb-tacked up. He could hardly believe what he read, "Retained on instructor status at Bartow Army Air Field 2nd Lt. Drew, Urban L. and 2nd Lt. Kemp, William T." He went straight to the Admin Office to protest. What he got was a speech on every man doing his duty.

In the morning, his first six, newly winged second lieutenants reported to him for training.

I had known Kemp briefly before this and he said, "Don't worry, Drew, maybe one or two classes at the most, and then they will send us to combat. Couple of months at most." How wrong he was.

Meanwhile, I did my best to make Mustang *combat pilots out of my students. I had my share of good ones... and bad ones. Some you had to work harder with than others, but in the long run, all of my students graduated. In hindsight, those days at Bartow were the best thing that happened to me. The best way to really learn is to teach.*

At Bartow, they flew aerial or ground gunnery, or both, every day. They flew against each other learning combat tactics. First, one versus one. On subsequent flights the number of airplanes increased until there were a dozen fighters in a tumultuous dogfight. They flew hours of formation. They flew across Florida, Georgia and the Gulf of Mexico honing navigation skills. They learned the *Mustang* inside and out.

The neophyte fighter pilots were allotted sixty hours for training. The instructors flew the syllabus again and again. Starting anew with each class.

The months went by; four, five, six, seven. Ben thought he would surely miss the war. Each month, he, and Kemp, submitted a request for combat duty. Each month, it came back. "Request denied,... needed as instructors, regret unable..."

They also flew other types of aircraft while towing the long sleeve for an aerial gunnery target. There was a stable of odd types at Bartow. Ben flew what were originally the navy's SBD *Dauntless*, the air force called it the A-24, and the SB2C *Helldiver*, redesignated A-25, and a clapped-out, early air corps P-47 *Thunderbolt*. It broadened his experience and feel for a variety of airplanes.

As their confidence grew, Drew and Kemp both again walked the edge. A couple of buzz jobs earned them a month as operators of the skeet range. A mild punishment which turned into an asset. Shooting skeet develops the shooting "eye". There is no better training for deflection shooting from a cockpit than blasting arcing clay pigeons. Only a few fighter pilots were any good at deflection shooting. Kemp and Drew became very adept at it – they both could shortly shoot 25's at least every other round on the skeet range.

But what the hell were we doing sitting on the northern edge of the Everglades, teaching young pilots to fly and fight. Were we ever to get to combat? We just didn't known what to do. We were drinking too much, chasing too many women, staying out too late... and we were making our unhappiness known to senior officers.
We had to get out of there.

One morning I was scheduled to take three lieutenants to the ground gunnery range at Indian Rocks in the Gulf. After take off, one of them aborted due to a rough engine, a second one aborted due to radio failure and finally the third one aborted for who knows what reason. So there I was with no students... and a full load of ammunition. I went to the ground range in a foul mood, shot off my rounds and headed back home on the deck. I wasn't really paying attention to where I was.
Next thing I know, there's this airfield right over my spinner. There's rows of airplanes, troops lined up at attention and a fancy reviewing stand, full of people. It's way too late to turn away. Besides, if I turn or climb they'll be able to read my number. If I stay low enough, and go straight over the top, no one will be able to tell who I was.
Or so I thought. It was one of those snap decisions you regret as soon as they are made.

I held the Mustang *down. The entire reviewing party and the front four ranks of troops hit the ground. I really laid them out.*

As much as he may have rationalized flying low and close over the troops to avoid detection, a more likely explanation was in Ben's subconscious.

The defining trait of a true fighter pilot is aggressiveness. Yet, there he was; trained to a fine edge, ready and eager for combat and assigned training duties in sunny, quiet Florida. How much was boredom a factor? Frustration at not being in combat? Was he overwhelmed by feeling stuck in cushy peace while the war went on without him?

Whatever the reason, conscious or not, Ben flattened the troops and angered Colonel Cochrane. The dangerous stunt got him the change he was seeking. Although for the next days he would go through personal hell in fear of losing all he had gained.

The CO and the Ops Officer were both waiting. Ben never had a chance to try the excuses he had concocted on the way back. He had not buzzed just any field. He had flown over Drane Field in Lakeland. He had not flattened just any reviewing party, but Colonel "Flip" Cochrane's. Already famous throughout the Air Force, Colonel Cochrane was conducting the final passing out parade before his Group left for the China-Burma-India Theater. He was furious.

The sergeant of the guard arrived with a Jeep and took Ben to his room. He was under quarters arrest, awaiting formal proceedings to convene a general court martial. He was in deep and serious trouble this time.

Ben did not sleep well that night. Death row in a penitentiary was a more cheerful place.

The next morning as the sergeant brought his food tray, he saw there was a second meal on the rolling cart. Ben asked who the other breakfast was for. "Oh, didn't you know, Sir?" the sergeant said, "Your buddy Lieutenant Kemp is also under quarters arrest and up for a court martial. Seems there was an altercation in some night club in Lakeland the other night over a young lady and Lieutenant Kemp fractured the jaw of an infantry captain."

After three days of agony, worry and excruciating boredom, Lieutenants Drew and Kemp were at the group commander's office in class-A uniforms at 0600. The sun was barely above the horizon. Condemned men at dawn. They were escorted in and hit a cadet brace they held for the next thirty minutes. Colonel Ward Harker never did tell them to stand at ease.

"Are you gentlemen familiar with the 104th Article of War? It is a form of discipline short of a court martial. The commanding officer is the judge, jury and executes the sentence. In a general court martial, your side of the story would be brought out. That is, if either of you had anything worth saying. Under the 104th Article of War, I can exercise discipline with no course to testimony from the accused. Do you understand?"

Drew and Kemp nodded and muttered, "Yessir."

"I am making a 104th Article entry in both your records. Which, to say the least, will assure that you two screw-ups will be the longest serving lieutenants in the history of this man's Air Force. Do you understand?"

Drew and Kemp nodded again and said, "Yessir. No questions, Sir."

"If I brought either of these violations of regulations to the attention of the Wing, you both would, without a doubt, be court-martialed and drummed out of the service. Do you understand that very clearly?"

Drew and Kemp were linked automatons, barely breathing. They nodded their heads in unison. Colonel Harker stared at them until they said "Yessir" through dry mouths.

"I am sorely tempted to let you go to court-martial." He paused and looked at the papers on his desk while his words sank in. Drew and Kemp were rigid.

"However, you two are probably the best instructors we have ever had in this unit, and that includes some of the combat veterans. Both of you could be superb fighter pilots. Drew, three of your students are already aces and, Kemp, one of yours also." The praise confused them, although they dared not show it.

Colonel Harker loudly called for the Sergeant of the Guard and his squadron clerk. They were in his office within seconds – long seconds to Kemp and Drew. "Cut orders for these two lieutenants immediately." He emphasized the low rank. " Send them over to the Eighth Air Force. Maybe getting shot at will teach them how to behave. I want them off this base within 24 hours. Get them out of here before higher headquarters asks me why I didn't recommend convening a pair of general courts martial."

Outside the CO's door, Bill Kemp and I couldn't help grinning at each other. We had gotten our combat assignment! Sure, it was not the smartest way, and we hadn't done it that way intentionally, but we were on our way to England.

It had been a tense, worried couple of days for me, and I know it was the same for Billy. Perhaps that shared anxiety is why Kemp and I became good friends.

The Replacement Pilot Center, the "Pool", was in Tallahassee, Florida, and we rode a bus there. Usually, it was a trip of only a couple of hours, but we stopped at several bars along the way. We had a piano player aboard the bus, who had played with Harry James, and he'd play when whatever bar we were in had a piano. I sing pretty well; as did some of the other guys on the bus. We had everyone going before we were halfway. Billy kept taking friendly punches at my arm. Even playing around, when Kemp punches, you stay punched. Both my upper arms were black and blue in the morning.

By the time we arrived at Tallahassee, the whole busload of young men leaving for war was in a most liquid condition. Kemp had climbed on top of the bus with the baggage and was singing Oh Solo Mio *more than slightly off key when we dragged him down at the gate to the base.*

Besides a couple, or three, drinking evenings chasing coeds from the university, there wasn't much for us to do. I couldn't help but think how much I had changed. When I arrived in Bartow with my shiny new wings, I was a virgin, figuratively and literally. Had never drunk a drop of alcohol. The first time I got laid was in the back seat of a local girl's car. Must have sounded like an idiot afterwards. "If you're pregnant, I'll marry you. I'll marry you. I promise. If you're pregnant, I'll do the right thing." Learned soon afterwards she'd probably slept with most of the Mustang *pilots who went through Bartow. She wasn't a pro or anything, just one of those girls caught up in wartime do-anything-for-our-boys. Now here I was chasing skirts and boozing it up every night.*

It was a happy time. I was on my way to what I wanted to do most. If I had known how bad my next experiences would be, I wouldn't have been quite so carefree.

2 Lt. Urban, "Ben", Drew as an instructor in the *Mustang* RTU, Bartow, Florida. The insignia on the tail of the P-51 is of the 56 Fighter Squadron of the 54 Fighter Group.

10

BOTTISHAM

It's a Long Way to Tipperary

The train left Tallahassee at midnight. Crammed six to a compartment, the would-be warriors watched the sun rise, and set again, before getting off at Camp Kilmer. What was left of that night, and yet another in the thrown together clapboard barracks blended in seamless misery with the monotony and discomfort of the long train ride. Their stay in the receiving center barracks with wood so new it oozed pine sap, was mercifully short.

The sun had barely lit the New Jersey Pine Barrens, when the pilots, navigators and bombardiers heading for England loaded their heavy luggage on an olive drab painted bus for the three hour ride to Manhattan. All they saw of New York City was through dirty windows on the drive to the Hudson River piers. Tied up there was the Cunard liner, *Queen Elizabeth*. Her grey painted bow was visible for only minutes before the bus turned left into the giant shed that covered all of Pier 90. The lines to check in and get their room assignments were long and slow. The lines up the covered gangways were long and slow.

When they learned the name of this great, grey ship, their hopes rose. No slow barge of a transport for these gentlemen and officers. They were going for a cruise on the epitome of luxury afloat. Or so they thought.

Their expectation was understandable. Until the Autumn of 1939, France's *Normandie* and the British Cunard liner, *Queen Mary*, were *The* way to travel across the Atlantic. In 1942 during conversion to a troopship, *Normandie* had a disastrous fire and had capsized at the next pier to where the Cunard liners tied up. It had taken a year to right her and she was taken to the Brooklyn yards for repair. The *Normandie* never sailed again.

The *Queen Mary* had had three dazzling years pampering passengers across the Atlantic. It was easy to confuse her with her sister ship, *Queen Elizabeth*. The second Queen was intended to be even more luxurious than her famous sister, but the outbreak of war found her incomplete in a fitting out dock on the Clyde River. Because of tides there were only two dates a half year apart when she could sail. She was rushed to minimum seaworthiness. A complex ruse was set up to deceive the Germans into thinking she was bound for Southampton and sea trials. On 26 February, 1940, *Queen Elizabeth*, was carefully towed down river to the Firth of Clyde where she loaded her life boats and other equipment that had been left off to give more clearance across the sand bars. Her Captain received his sealed, and most secret, sailing orders. *Queen Elizabeth* headed out onto the cold North Atlantic.

Five days later, she sailed into New York Harbor and a tumultuous welcome. She had been carrying troops to war ever since.

For non-sailors, ships are great, confusing labyrinths of passageways and ladders. For Ben Drew, Bill Kemp and all the other hotshots, eager to get to the war, the *Queen Elizabeth* was more waiting in lines, more forms, more pieces of paper. One of those pieces of paper told them where they would sleep, where they would live, where and when they would eat for the next week. The paper was very specific; it had in great detail directions for how to find their stateroom.

Queen Elizabeth was filled with bewildered airmen walking the passages, heavy B-4 bags in hand, asking anyone who vaguely looked like he knew his way around, where the hell, stateroom so and so was. On a ship 1,031 feet long and 110 feet wide it was possible to walk for miles without getting anywhere.

Eventually, of course, Ben found his assigned room.

The plate on the door was polished brass, the number recessed and painted with black enamel. The door was richly polished wood; mahogany. The knob was also polished brass. Inside, the Queen's elegance was reflected in pastel paint and more mahogany trim. On a bulkhead near the doorway was a discrete sign intended to advise passengers of a happier time, that this room was for a maximum of four persons.

Ben was a reasonably early arrival. Of course, he was surprised to find four other officers already there, and had no sooner introduced himself, when three more came in. Then two more, a larger gaggle of five, and two, and a last straggler.

If any of them had stopped to consider the dozen ugly, three inch, steel pipes welded to deck and overhead, with three sets of steel hooks welded to the pipes, they would have realized that this was no longer a room for four persons, but eighteen officers of the United States Army Air Forces.

Folded vertically, were metal frames with canvas laced inside, and a thin mattress. The chains which supported the beds when opened were out of sight. They were called "standee bunks" and made it possible to get 16,000 men on board.

It would be a long week.

No more than three of them could get dressed at the same time. They waited in line for the latrine; which they rapidly learned on a ship was called a head. Sea sickness was a disaster. When the weather was bad, there was room inside only for standing. The other choice was to lie in your bunk. If one man farted, every man breathed the stench. It was communal living of the worst sort. There were no secrets.

What would have been the Queen's luxurious dining rooms were turned into army chow halls. Instead of monogrammed silver, there were stamped, steel mess kits that had the dessert Jello melting from the heat of the "mystery meat" and inevitable mashed potatoes. Where the captain's table was to have hosted honored passengers, fifty men sat at a trestle table and bolted their food to make room for the men behind them. Late and early sittings gave way to a continuous line which wound up to the next deck. Each man was restricted to two meals a day by more pieces of paper. The etched glass lamps and wood paneling a snickering reminder of travel "before the war."

The good news was she was fast. Soldiers on transports like the "Liberty Ships" lived in the same pitiful conditions and took twice the time to cross in a zigzagging convoy. *Queen Elizabeth* traveled at a speed of 35 knots and could out run the German U-boats... or so they were told. The Queen did not zig and zag, after all, it was undignified. Her speed would keep her safe. This scared the hell out of everyone.

They would have been more frightened if they knew there was space in the lifeboats for only half of them. A decision made when the *Queens* started carrying American GI's to England, was to double the "safe" complement "because of the war."

Those officers with the foresight to bring along a bottle or two of Rye or Bourbon were extremely popular with their cabin mates. And woe betide any officer who thought he could keep his booze hidden for himself.

Among the air force types, there were constant rumors of regular army officers screwing nurses on deck at night. None of them ever saw the act itself, but readily believed it was true. The infantry, armor and artillery officers griped about the air corps glory boys being the ones who had the nurses. Neither, in actuality, saw much of the nurses; the few women onboard were kept strictly in their own sections of the ship. They complained that despite so many men on board, they were living in a seagoing convent.

After six days of interminable card and dice games, meaningless conversations, waiting in one line or another, and an occasional drink of whiskey, the men had their first glimpse of Scotland as *Queen Elizabeth* steamed up the River Clyde and docked at Gourock, the port of the city of Glascow.

Any expectations of an exotic, foreign, postcard land were destroyed by the grubby, grey, buildings, docks and machinery of a working port. Early in the war, when fear of invasion was high, teams of Royal Army Engineers had taken the cranes and heavy equipment from the Channel ports which normally served the great ocean liners and moved them to ports in Scotland which were out of reach of *Luftwaffe* bombers. The appearance of the machinery was the last thing those engineers cared about. Making it work was their aim. The machinery, and docks, and surrounding town looked it.

The sun was shining, but there was a grey pall of smoke from a dozen ships' funnels, coal burning power plants, foundries, and households ashore.

The bus that carried them to the railroad station added its share to the miasma of smoke. It had been modified by the addition of a huge, coal fired boiler which hung like a leech on its back. Petrol was scarce... and needed at the front. A train took them to the Eighth Air Force Receiving Center at Stone in Staffordshire.

Two hundred men crowded into a small amphitheater in a grey sided building with a green roof. Originally a warehouse, flimsy partitions and thin walls had divided its high ceilinged spaces into offices and rooms large enough for crowds of men. They all had orders to the Eighth Air Force, but nothing more specific than that. Each man was eager to learn his fate, but would have to wait. Somewhere, sometime, in the mayhem that was the receiving center, an assignment to a Group would be given to him. After traveling to wherever the Group currently was, he would be assigned a Squadron. Once in the Squadron, if a fighter pilot, he would be put in a Flight.. But first, they had to be officially welcomed.

The officer tasked with welcoming them was only a first lieutenant so he could not call the group to attention because a quarter of them were senior to him. "Gentlemen," he called loudly, "gentlemen. If I could have your undivided attention."

The Lieutenant waited until the room was completely still. He did not smile. "Welcome to the Eighth Air Force."

Ben was sitting in a middle row. He leaned over to Bill Kemp, "Isn't that an Air Medal he's wearing?"

"Yeah, it sure is. Thought you only wore the ribbon except for ceremonies?"

"Exactly. Maybe he's trying to impress us."

"I'd be more impressed if I knew what he's done."

The Lieutenant on the small stage did not explain who he was or where he was from, but went on, "while you've been at home, we have been fighting a war over here. We have invaded Europe. The Hun, gentlemen, is a vicious opponent and will fight all the harder now that we are on his home field. The American cemeteries in England are filling up... but there's always room for more. I am guessing that only one out of ten of you will be alive in thirty days."

Kemp, a little too loudly, asked Ben, "Who is this total asshole?"

"I don't know buddy, but let's get the hell out of here and get where somebody wants to fight."

The Lieutenant droned on in his despondent way about listening to the veterans and following regulations and obeying senior officers and how bad it was going to be. Small jokes and asides could soon be heard from all over the hall. The scratchy PA which had been making sporadic, half intelligible announcements since they had first walked into the center stopped the Lieutenant's litany of gloom.

"Screeee.. LIEUTENANTS DREW AND KEMP REPORT TO DESK SEVEN. ssscrreeee. Click. THAT IS, sscreee-AWK...ANTS DREW 'N KEMP TO DESK SEVEN. Sssssss."

The two of them needed no urging. With big grins on their faces, they stepped over feet and legs to move down the row of chairs. The Lieutenant with the medal waited patiently until he thought he had his captive audience's complete attention. He, of course, did not, as most were busy wondering why Drew and Kemp had been singled out.

Desk seven was hard to find. A crowd of airmen blocked the large piece of cardboard with a black stenciled 7 hung on the front of the desk. There was a line, but the two men who should have been next were talking to each other, so Ben and Bill pushed past them to the edge of the desk.

The desk's collapsible stand was pulled out with a typewriter on it. Four piles of mixed flimsies, manila folders and envelopes left a narrow space in the center of the desk. A sergeant sat with his head down studying a list of three columns.

Despite having been in the service almost exactly the same length of time, Ben Drew and Bill Kemp had developed very different attitudes towards the sergeants they encountered.

Kemp stood leaning forward with his right arm straight and clenched fist on the desk corner. Drew was practically at attention in the exact center as he said, "Sergeant, here we are. That is, Lieutenants Drew and Kemp reporting as instructed. May we help you, Sir ?"

The sergeant looked up with one eyebrow raised. "Sonny, no need to kiss my ass, I don't need it."

Kemp jerked his hand up. Before he could say anything, the sergeant continued, " Normally, we kinda just pull numbers out of the hat, so to speak, and send you wet-behind-the-ears, junior birdmen, to whatever group we please. To wherever there's an opening." He waved his hand over the six inch piles on his desk. "But today, I got a special request. Pain in the ass." He resumed studying the list in front of him.

When he did not look up again, Kemp's hand went back into a fist against his chest and he began to twist his wrist. Ben raised his hand and lightly touched his friend's sleeve. "Um, sergeant, could you please tell us where we are going, Sir?"

"Lissen' sonny, you don't call me sir. I ain't no officer." He moved a four page list and picked up a scrap of paper with a penciled note on it. "Pain in the ass. You guys know someone, or what?"

"No Sir, no sergeant, we don't know what's going on..."

"Dammit," Kemp growled, "just tell us where we're going."

The sergeant stared at Kemp who was now patting his fist with his left palm. "Special request. You two are headed for the 361st Fighter Group. 'Yellowjackets', or some la-de-da thing. Pain in the ass." He picked up his list again.

"That's it? That's all?", said Ben.

"Listen, I'll give you a real pain in the ass," said Kemp, leaning on straight arms, both fists clenched on the desk, "if you don't get helpful. Real quick."

"OK, OK." The sergeant opened the center drawer, pulled out a folder and slowly read, "361st Fighter Group. Bottisham Air Base. East Anglia. England."

"We know it's in England. Where in England? How do we get there?"

"I'd take a train if I were you. It's a hell of a walk."

"Lissen, smartass, a train to where? When do we go? How about some tickets? Where are our orders?"

"One at a time, sonny. Your orders went out by courier today. You can't get tickets without orders. Looks like you'll have to buy your own. I'd leave as soon as possible, someone must really want you there. And I have no idea where Bottisham is. There's over a hundred bases on this island. Ask at the station. Now, get out of here, I've got better things to do."

Ben pulled Bill Kemp all the way onto the street.

The ancient, black, taxi cab squealed to a stop at the red and white striped pole that marked the entrance to the Bottisham airbase. Bottisham had been an RAF station since the start of the war and was now on loan to the Americans "for the duration". The guard post was a solid brick building, not one of the flimsy boxes at the newly built bases.

An American PFC stood on the left side of the road near the counter weight for the pole. He pushed his green helmet with stenciled white MP's on the sides comfortably back and put his head near the open window as he asked the old cabby, "And just who might you be?"

From the back seat, Ben said, "Private, we are pilots reporting to this base."

Kemp was not so patient. The run-in with the sergeant at the replacement center must of reminded him of uses for military protocol. That, or he was simply tired and annoyed from the train and cab rides. He jumped out the right side door. "Private. Is this how you talk to officers? Did you forget how to salute?"

The PFC straightened to attention. His helmet fell off. He bent to pick it up. Decided to salute first. He straightened again and shakily saluted. He bent down again and lifted his helmet in his hand.

"PRIVATE!"

Startled, he dropped the helmet, stood straight and saluted again. "Sorry, Sir, Lieutenant sir."

"Listen you sad sack, we're here to fight a war. You read me, private? You get that pole up damn quick or you'll be in a foxhole in France in two shakes."

"Yessir, rightawaysir." He grabbed his helmet and jammed it on with one hand, pushed the pole up with the other. As the taxi drove past, he was at a brace, right arm in a rigid salute, left hand on the counterweight. He couldn't hear Kemp and Drew laughing.

Captain Larry Houston, was the 375th squadron's intelligence officer. Before the war, he was a practicing attorney in New York City. Older than the pilots he briefed and debriefed, he provided some sense of mature guidance, although he was only in his late 20's himself. He got along well with most of them. Eventually, even with Ben Drew, despite their bad beginning.

The pair had paid the cabby by the time honored method of holding out a handful of notes and coins and saying take what you need. It was a lot simpler that way for two boys raised in middle America than figuring out pounds, pence, shillings and the even stranger slang terms the cabby used. Most of the time this method works quite well as the locals are so amazed at the level of naive trust, they do not think of cheating such innocence.

They dumped their heavy bags near the door and searched for someone to check in with. A flight sergeant told them Captain Houston was the only officer in the admin building. His office was next to the briefing room down the hall on the left.

Houston was sorting previous mission reports when they walked in, but he was glad to put them aside and become, as he said, the first to officially welcome them. They did not tell him about the bemedaled first lieutenant at the Stone Depot. Colonel Christian wasn't available, but he'd take them to their quarters and they could see the group CO after they unpacked.

Houston drove them in an open topped Jeep and pointed out which building was what as they came in sight. Bottisham was a mix of tunnel-like Nissen huts and painted wooden structures thrown up fast by the USAAF. A two story, square, operations building with a control tower on the roof was the highest on the base.

Kemp's quarters were first. Ben and Captain Houston helped him move his gear into a four man room in a standard US, GI built Nissen hut barracks. No surprise there.

Ben was some distance away; in one of the frame buildings. Ben was surprised by how nice the interior was. It was the most militarily elegant quarters he had ever seen. The previous occupants had been officers of the Royal Air Force. These Brits know how to live, he thought. He was about to find out just how well.

Larry Houston was a friendly man. His job showed him more of the character and personality of the pilots than anyone else could learn. At times he wished it did not. He knew who the good shots were, who were true leaders; who was brave and who was a liar. He knew the braggarts and cheaters; the talkers and the doers. He learned the cowards... and the heroes. He had an honest and just outlook on life. In the American legal system he had worked in, a man was innocent until proven guilty. Transposed to new pilots, his attitude became, each was a hero until proven otherwise. He carried one of Ben's bags into the second room on the right.

"Drew there is your bed. You're the fourth pilot in five weeks to sleep in it. The others are all dead."

"Listen you ground-pounder, whatever you are," Ben snapped, "I'll be in this godamned bed, until I choose to leave it, and not before. Why don't you haul ass out of here."

Houston was startled by the reaction; he had only stated a fact. He dealt in facts; enemy engaged, rounds fired, aircraft destroyed. He looked sadly at this newcomer. Gently lowered the bag to the floor. "A Jeep will come get you at 0800 hours. The group CO will see you then."

He stared at a silent Second Lieutenant Urban Drew for a another moment, turned slowly and left the room. He left the door open.

Ben pondered what the last minutes meant. Why had he said that? It was stupid. A bad beginning. Was he more nervous than he would admit to himself?

He was listlessly taking clothes out of the B-4 bag spread open on his bed, when a voice from behind him said, "May I assist you sir?"

His mind still on his gaffe with Houston, Ben jumped around with his arm out defensively. A man wearing a high collared, green tunic with the broad stripes of a British corporal stepped, leaned back.

"Sorry, sir. Din't mean to startle."

"Who the hell are you?"

"I, sir, am your batman, of course."

"And, just what is a batman?"

"Well, sir, I press your uni-form, make tea in the mornin', do tha laundry, make up tha bed, keep your things tidy..."

"Like a butler?"

"Oh noo, sir. A butler is much, much more. 'E's concerned with the whole house. 'E's a gentlemun's gentlemun. In civvie terms, I'm more like a manservant. Like I said, I generally do whatever you ask me to."

"Well, butler or batman, sounds like a good deal to me. Carry on my man. I'm very glad to have you."

As his batman organized his things, Ben thought of the tales the veterans brought back to Bartow of life in New Guinea, Guadalcanal, North Africa. Tales of dust, or mud; water that had to be boiled, atabrine tablets for malaria which turned your skin livid yellow, scavenging wood to make a floor in the tent you erected yourself... and erected again after each windstorm. Tales of showers with cold, or sun warmed water, of primitive laundries pounding shirts with rocks until they shredded after a few weeks. Of heat so bad the pilots made shorts of their khaki pants by hacking off the legs with a knife. The same food three times a day for weeks on end. Thank you, God, he said to himself, I'm just where I want to be.

His pampered days lasted only a month. It was long enough to get used to having a manservant so when deprived of the luxury, he bitched loud and long. To no avail. The Royal Air Force bureaucracy realized, finally, that Bottisham was no longer their base and withdrew all their remaining personnel. Of course, Ben and the small fraction of American airmen who had had batmen got no sympathy, whatsoever, from their squadron mates.

The officers of 375th Fighter Squadron, Bottisham, late July, 1944
(Names in **boldface** appear in the book)
Back row: Spaulding, Boelter, Morgan, Eason, Bell, **Cole**, **Edwards**, Shackleford, **Bill Kemp**, **Bill McCoppin**, **"Doc" Emlaw**, Cowle, Gill, Genteler, **"Red" Rowlett**.
Short row: Narvis and Kapre
Middle row: Comer, Snyder, Adams, **Armsby**, Wright, Ewert, Black, **Roswell Freedman**, Hall, Ben Drew.
Front row: Donahue, **Bill Rogers**, Thomas, Sobieski, **Rainey**, Morehouse, Neeley, **Frank Glankler**.
In front: **Major Cummins**, "Snitz" the mascot, **Martin Johnson**

The next morning Drew and Kemp met the commanding officer of the 361st Fighter Group for the first time. The meeting was remarkable as much because of the man as for what he had to say. Colonel Christian at that time was the only West Point graduate commanding a fighter group in the Eighth Air Force. Colonel Christian managed to be casual without being sloppy, friendly without becoming familiar. He bridged the gap between colonel and second lieutenant in a way that made them feel welcome, but still aware of their position. Of course, after the scrapes they had been in, Drew and Kemp half expected to be in a brace in front of any senior officer. Instead they sat comfortably in large wood chairs with arms while Colonel Christian explained why they were there.

"The two of you are probably wondering why you were asked for." They nodded their heads. They were wondering why they had been paged at the replacement center in Stone. "I have a problem I believe you may help solve. One of the squadrons in this group, the 375th, has had some serious losses. Lieutenant Colonel George Merritt was the only ace in this group. He was the commanding officer of the 375th and, a few days ago, he was lost. Last week, Captain John Guyckeson, who also went to West Point, was lost." As he continued his litany, Colonel Christian stared above his new pilots' heads as he remembered the faces of the lost men. "In the last ten days, two of four flight commanders were lost to enemy action. It's kind of gloomy over there. Morale in the 375th is almost zero."

The colonel gazed at the middle distance for a few moments, shook his head, smiled and passed his hand over the two manila folders in the center of his desk. " I asked around at headquarters and your names came up. I have your two personal files here. The pair of you have quite a record." He let the thought hang while the second lieutenants wondered which way the conversation would go. He was smiling, so it couldn't be bad… could it?

"You two probably have more time in the P-51 *Mustang* than any pilot on this base. Some of this group's pilots are former students of yours and they are all doing well. You may be junior in rank, but you're long on experience. I am assigning you to the 375th. Major Freeman is a good CO and Martin Johnson, who is our leading strafer, is there, but you two just may provide the boost the squadron needs." He stood. Their welcome speech was almost over. They rose to go.

Colonel Christian spoke again. "You'll start out as all replacements do, but if you are half as good as your reputations, you can expect to be flight leaders before too long."

Kemp and Drew's grins may have reminded him of what else was in their folders, because he waited until they were at the door before he added, "If you perform as I think you can," he paused, "and you stay out of trouble. I just may, perhaps, decide to remove this little entry of the 104th article of war from your records." Colonel Christian's grin was as wide as theirs.

"Dismissed. And good luck."

11

TOUSSUS-LE NOBLE

First Time

I think too much is made of a pilot's first mission. At least, it was in my case. Sure, I was probably nervous. More a matter of wanting to not screw up, than fear. To be afraid, you have to know what's going on. Later, I was afraid, but not that first time. Hell, it was what I had been trained for – it was what I wanted to do. What I wanted all those months at Bartow. It was also a heck of a busy flight. All firsts are busy. There is so much to see, so much that's new. It didn't take me long to settle in – I already knew the airplane like an old friend – but radio procedures, the terrain, what did France look like, flying wing, becoming part of the team. That was the hard part. I was lucky too that that first one went as well as it did.

Kemp and Billy Rogers had flown their first missions two days earlier and I was champing at the bit. I flew in the number two position on Martin Johnson's wing. Johnny was the A flight commander at the time. He had racked up a bunch of kills, but they were all on the ground. He was a good flight leader and experienced; he was about to complete his tour.

We escorted 160 Liberators over Paris. The escort portion of the mission was easy. I found I could easily fly wing and keep my scan going. It was interesting to see the bombers up close, in formation, in flight. I hadn't ever flown alongside more than two or three at one time before then. Didn't see *any enemy fighters at all. No one in the entire group did. A small part of my brain gloated that now that the Germans knew Urban Drew had arrived, they'd stay away. Right.*

Anyway, the "heavies" dropped their loads on an airdrome to the southwest of Paris, near Chartres. Our flight, Cadet Yellow, *was designated as the "spotter flight" that day. While the rest of the group stayed up at 25,000 feet, we dropped down to 2,000 feet to observe the bombers' hits. It was impressive. Five hundred pounder after five hundred pounder exploded in a torrent of dirt and smoke. I could feel the shock waves come off of each bomb. I don't know how men on the ground could stand such an attack. The bombers hit the southeast corner of the field and had a nice tight bomb pattern.*

As we circled, Johnson noticed that the adjoining airdrome of Toussus-Le Noble had airplanes parked all over the place. We climbed briefly into the clouds to confuse the ground gunners. In the cloud, of course, all I could see was the lead aircraft. He was flying on instruments for all of us. We just hung in there and matched the motion of his aircraft. After a minute, we dropped down into bright sunshine. We loosened the formation so we could each look around. Johnson had us perfectly lined up on some revetments on the far side of the field. We kept dropping lower and strafed the machine shops and work sheds in the buildings. It was great. I felt like I was back on the practice range in Florida. I saw hits, but couldn't tell if anything caught fire or not.

Flying low, at high speed, all your senses are sharpened. Flying the airplane becomes automatic and there is a perception of detail. One shed had a corrugated roof. The door to the next was open. I stopped firing when the buildings got too close. Looked over at Johnson; checked his position. Looked back forward.

There, smack on my nose, was a Junkers 52 in a revetment. The trimotor looked cocky sitting there. I let loose with a burst and observed my fire going into the fuselage and wing roots. Just as I passed over, I saw an orange blob of flame come up and I think it caught fire. Rosenberger was behind me and he confirmed that it burned. Captain Johnson also shot up a plane in its revetment and it too burned. Lieutenant Jack Crandell was the number four man and he got yet another Ju52.

Flak was moderate while we were over the airdrome and increased as we tried to get away. Jack Crandell took a Flak hit in his right wing just outside his outboard gun. The hole slowed him down, but he finally caught up and slid into formation, just in time for our flight to chase some Me109s. They were too far away to catch before they climbed into the overcast at about 3,000 feet and didn't come back out. We headed for the Channel and made it home OK. I had fired 338 rounds and the mission lasted two hours and forty-five minutes. My first combat.

When Kemp saw the combat film, he said, "Drew, I don't give you any credit at all for that Junkers. I don't count aircraft sitting on ground. The Eighth Air Force might, but I sure don't. Let me know when you get a real score. And that's that."

This was the beginning of what was to go on between Billy Kemp and myself for the rest of our combat tour. There was the official credit list and our personal one. You can imagine which had the tougher criteria.

And Kemp wasn't the only one. Even my flight leader commented, "Well, Drew, don't be overly proud. First of all, it was on the ground. Secondly, you couldn't miss it. I had you aimed right at it."

I said, "Yes Sir, Captain Johnson, Sir, but it still counts as a victory."

"Yeah, I know, dammit, and I even signed the confirmation on it.

"I suppose I ought to say congratulations."

Bottisham was an air base only for World War Two. It's existence almost matched the duration of hostilities. It was typical of many bases in England.

Cambridgeshire is farming country. The land is generally flat with gentle slopes for drainage. The great forests from the time of Robin Hood were long gone. Cleared for crops and pasturage. Small copses remained; hardly worthy of the name forest. Hedgerows and rock walls jigsaw across the land dividing property. It was simple for the Royal Air Force to acquire a tract of suitable land. Existing buildings in Bottisham village provided quarters for the officers. The RAF built more as barracks for the enlisted men. The manor house belonging to the Jensyn family became senior officers quarters. As the Group commander, Colonel Christian lived there as did Lieutenant Colonel Joe Kruzel who was his deputy and successor. Part of the arrangement was that a family grandmother be allowed to stay in the house. The somewhat eccentric old lady had her own rooms and whenever she happened on the air force officers, she would assume they were guests of her grandson.

A Macadam perimeter track with paved pads for the airplanes sprouting along the sides like buds on a branch was built first. The rich soil was bulldozed into berms around the pads to provide protective revetments. Grass seed was planted everywhere. There were no runways as was the custom at the start of the war. The grassy area inside the roughly pentagonally shaped track was used for take-off and alighting. Bottisham Royal Air Force Base went operational in 1940.

During the Battle of Britain, it became apparent that sod was unsuitable for the heavier and faster aircraft equipping front line squadrons, so pierced steel planking, PSP, was laid to form a runway. Then another runway was built and finally a third reached across the widest points of the pentagon. Each PSP runway was about 3,000 feet long.

When the United States Army Air Force began its buildup in late 1942, the planes of the newly formed USAAF Eighth Air Force needed space. Bottisham was turned over to the Americans in late 1943.

The American base was still called Bottisham, but officially it was USAAF Station 374#

As Ben Drew and a few lucky others with batmen had learned, the transition took some time.

In January, 1944, all the runways were widened with additional sections of PSP to allow flights of four fighters to take-off simultaneously. Additional hangars and facilities were added over the course of the war, but the PSP was slippery when wet and difficult to keep in shape, so Bottisham was never an ideal air base.

Ben flew an uneventful second mission, but on his third, only four days after his first, he went rampaging over the French countryside demonstrating that he possessed another important factor a successful fighter pilot needs – luck. The best shooting skills in the world are pointless if there are no worthwhile targets. He was in a flight of three *Mustangs* with Edwards and Raimee, which found an active railroad marshaling yard. Evidence from the gun camera credited new guy, Second Lieutenant U.L. Drew with destroying three locomotives, damaging six more, blowing five two-ton trucks to smithereens and clobbering a couple of river barges. He not only knew how to shoot straight, but keep his bursts short. He knew how to use enough ammo to do the job, but not a bullet more.

Bill Kemp drew his first blood the day after that. Like Ben's first, it was a ground kill; an *Me109* he strafed. As far as he was concerned, it was about time. Ben's bragging was getting on his nerves.

The score was one apiece.

12

LISIEAUX

First in the Air

The first few missions were really a case of starting out with a bang. The next batch were quiet by comparison. Heck, they were quiet, period. I used them mostly to learn my way around France. Even when hanging on to someone's wing and scanning for bandits, I had my map out and kept track of where we were. Memories of getting lost in Mississippi made me work constantly at navigation. Landing in some potato patch was nothing compared to getting lost over enemy territory. I knew how easy it was to get separated from a formation once a dogfight got started. Too many pilots got bagged by blundering across some German Flak *trap. I wasn't going to be one of them.*

Johnson was my flight leader for most of my early missions. He was a competent pilot and a good leader. Gruff at times, but I respected the man. He was late in his tour and had a batch of ground kills, but a kill in the air had eluded him. Despite the Eighth Air Force credits, any real fighter pilot wanted his victories in the air. Rickenbacker, and Guynemer, and Richtofen didn't count the planes they shot up on the ground. They were our heroes. They were the Aces. As I'll tell later, Johnson's desire for one in the air had some tragic consequences. The mission to Lisieux on June 25 certainly added to his frustration.

It was an early morning mission. We were in the assigned area around 0700 hours and spotted a flight of thirty plus. I followed Cadet Blue Leader, Captain Johnson, *down as the squadron attacked. We had been patrolling at 20,000 feet and the* Messerschmitts *were flying at 10,000 feet so we had plenty of speed and a good angle on them. When we bounced the formation, all hell broke loose. The Germans scattered all over the place. It was all I could do to hang on and stay in a position to keep Johnson's tail clear. If I was going to fly as a wingman, I was going to be a good one.*

Blue Leader had picked one lone 109 out for his target. When the pilot realized he was being chased, he hit the deck. He really got down in the tree tops. The poor bastard knew he was had. In the early days, the Messerschmitts *could outrun allied fighters so a straight course was the best to get away. The* Mustang *had so much speed that catching him wasn't a problem and he knew it, so he was maneuvering violently hoping to throw off our aim. A tall tree would pop up and he'd head for it, banking around at the last instant. He'd pop-over and duck back down at windbreak tree rows. He almost took the roof off of a couple of barns. He'd go straight sometimes for max speed then twist into another turn. He'd suddenly boot rudder and skid so from the back he looked like he was turning, but wasn't. He was no beginner and no easy target, but had wound up in a bad position without the equipment to get out of it. If I hadn't stuck with my leader, he might have made it.*

Johnson had not been using full power so he wouldn't overshoot. Time was on our side, so he was being careful. After about three minutes, but many miles, he was close enough to shoot. He squeezed the trigger and none of the guns in the right wing fired. The yaw caused by the three fifties in the left wing yawed the airplane unexpectedly and he missed. It was a moment any of us hated. There he was whipping over the French countryside at 300 miles an hour, less than a hundred feet up, trying to chase a zigzagging target and, at the same time, look down and recheck that all his armament switches were set correctly. He did look... and they were. Back in position, he fired again. The left guns popped off a dozen rounds and jammed again. The right guns never did fire.

Martin Johnson showed himself to be a true professional. The swearing and cursing going into his mask and running through his head was scathing, irreverent and profane. It would have peeled paint and wilted flowers. Every word of it was heartfelt and well deserved. However, all that went over the radio was a simple, "Take him, Blue Two."

Ben was higher and slightly behind when the call came. He pushed the throttle all the way forward and lowered his nose to close on the frantic *Messerschmitt*. Dead astern and one hundred yards out he opened fire. All four of his P-51B's guns fired. The distance closed rapidly – too rapidly. He had to pull up to avoid a collision. He pulled up a hundred feet and rolled to the right, dropping down on the German's tail once more.

One short burst finished the chase. A halo of pale yellow fire surrounded the slim fuselage. A few dark chunks flew off. The *Messerschmitt* started a somersault, but hit the ground before the nose went past vertical. The explosion made a blot of pieces of airplane and black dirt over a golden wheat field.

Martin Johnson got to confirm another kill by Ben Drew. An air kill.

June 25th was a good day for the Bottisham fliers. Besides, Ben's victory, Lieutenant Colonel Joe Kruzel got a *Focke-Wulf 190*, Lieutenant Crandell a pair of *109s* and Major Cummins another *Messerschmitt*.

So that's what it felt like. It was exhilarating. I flew home that afternoon as happy as I'd ever been. One on the ground and now one in the air, and I hadn't been in combat even two weeks. All those dreams over all those years... Now I knew. Knew I had what it takes. Knew I was going to be a successful fighter pilot. I wanted to fly every day. Rest meant nothing. I wanted to be posted on the ops board each day for the next day's missions.

I couldn't get enough flying in. Most of the guys wanted days off, but I didn't want to miss a shot at the Luftwaffe. I had come to fight, and that's what I wanted to do. It was all I wanted to do.

The score was Drew two, Kemp one.

Bill Kemp dressed for combat.
Bottisham Air Base, summer 1944

13

FRANCE

Bogey

BOGEY (pl:BOGIES): an unidentified contact in the air. Originally used for radar contacts, later for visual sightings as well. (Possible origin in folklore term *Bogey-man*.)

BANDIT: a radar or visual contact in the air which has been positively identified as enemy. Origin is self-explanatory. (Opposite is a FRIENDLY.)

Ben's reputation in the 375th squadron was growing. A ground kill on his first mission and an aerial kill on his sixth. On a mission at the start of July, his airplane was seriously damaged for the only time. His inexperience almost got him killed. His flying skill saved him. The episode should never have happened.

The "Yellow Jackets" of the 375th were on a patrol over France in squadron strength. There were sixteen *Mustang*s with yellow noses; a mix of B and new D models. They all had the E2 code on their sides. The formation leader that day was Captain Martin H. Johnson. He commanded A flight and was Ben's leader for most of his early missions. Because he was leading the squadron, his callsign was "Cadet Lead" while Ben was called "White Two".

The day was gray. The *Mustang*s were flying between two layers of clouds when a formation of two dozen aircraft descended in front of them from out of the overcast. The new formation consisted of single-engine, low wing, slim fuselage fighters. The *Mustang*s were in perfect position to attack.

"This is *Cadet Lead. Bandits*, Twelve o'clock."

"*Cadet Lead*, confirm they are bandits, not bogies."

"They're bandits, Twelve o'clock."

"*Cadet Leader*," another pilot in the formation attempted to clarify identification. Something did not look right. "Are you sure they're bandits?"

"They're bandits alright. Drop your tanks."

As ordered, sixteen pairs of partially full drop tanks tumbled away from the *Mustang*s, as their leader accelerated and closed in on the last airplane in the formation ahead.

The attack was perfect. A burst of 50 caliber exploded the aircraft into a ball of red flame and black smoke.

The Americans had been seen. The formation broke into their counter-attack. As the fighters turned hard in vertical banks, the *Mustang* pilots were shocked to recognize the graceful elliptical wings of RAF *Spitfires. Cadet Leader* had shot down a friendly. They rolled on to their backs and pulled hard into split-esses for the clouds below. All except one; Ben Drew.

I don't know what I was thinking about. Seemed like a good idea at the time. I intended to fly through their formation rocking my wings so the Brits could get a good look at the big star and bar on my wings. Show them it was all a mistake. A hell of a mistake, but mistake never the less. The Spitfire, our Mustangs *and the Messerschmitt 109 did all look alike from most angles. I was a friend. They wouldn't shoot at me.*

Next thing I knew, my control column was torn out of my hands and I was thrown over on my back in an inverted spin and felt a helluva shock and as I glanced out I could see a big hole in my left wing. One of the Spits had put a 20 millimeter shell in me.

I was pushed up in my straps. The sky was spinning. My head banging side to side. First step is to break the stall. Upside down that means pulling back on the control stick – opposite of a normal tailspin. And lots of rudder against the spin. The nose finally slewed up and around into an upright spin.

I reversed the rudder and popped the stick forward. The Mustang *recovered in another turn and I was pointed nose way down and airspeed building up fast. I'd lost a lot of altitude and the cloud deck was coming up fast. It took more force than usual on the ailerons to bring the wings level before I started pulling out.*

I didn't come all the way to level, but left the nose down and headed for the clouds. I needed to get away from one angry bunch of RAF pilots. I went into the soup at 2,500 feet. The terrain in that area is never more than a thousand so I started to level-off when my altimeter was just above that. Sure enough, I began seeing the ground. The cloud bottoms were about 800 feet. With all the cloud above, the day was dark and gloomy. I set max power before my airspeed could bleed off and looked around. Typical French countryside. There were no landmarks, just farm houses and fields, so I turned northwest for the Channel. I did a couple of quick turns to check my six.

I couldn't believe it. A couple of Spitfires *had followed my crazy dive through the clouds. They sat back at my seven and five o'clock. Didn't budge. If I turned, they turned. Shadowing me. My back kept tensing up waiting for the bullets.*

At the speed we were traveling, it didn't take long to reach the coast and I recognized where I was. I adjusted my heading to almost due north for Bottisham in Cambridgeshire. The pair of Spits turned right along with me. This scared the hell out of me because most of the RAF fighter bases were in Southern England; Sussex, or Kent. These wanted a piece of yours truly.

The clouds cleared over The Channel and I started a climb so I could raise Colgate Base on the radio sooner than normal. Told them I needed help. To get the MP's out. Have them waiting when I landed... and make sure they were armed. Got an acknowledgment. Guy on the radio sounded puzzled, but said the Military Police would be ready.

Back near my homebase now and knowing help was waiting, I got cocky. I'd show the Limeys how the Army Air Force flew. I kept my P-51 low and fast over the runway and did a pitch-up for landing rather than a sedate straight-in approach. Pulled up and rolled hard to make it look good. Damned, if they didn't follow right after me. Landed too.

By the time the Spitfires touched down, I was in the squadron parking area and shutdown. A whole truckload of MP's armed with M-1's was there. As well as a fair sized crowd of our people. Word of my unusual radio call had apparently gotten around. Thankfully, the request for MP's was taken seriously.

The Spitfires cleared the runway and were taxiing in our direction with that funny, bouncing gait that airplane had. Especially when taxied fast. The first one stopped, side on to us, about a hundred feet away. The canopy was open. The pilot pushed his goggles up and looked at my airplane and the truckload of GI's with the big white MP painted on their helmets. His head swung back and forth between the two. He made a decision and his arm went straight up in the air. I couldn't see what his fingers were doing, but I'm sure it wasn't a salute.

He gunned his engine hard enough to lift the Spit's tailwheel off the ground and spun around. His wingman never stopped rolling, but followed his leader back out to the runway. As he came by, his left arm shot up in the air too.

We all guessed what came next.

As the Spitfires broke ground, their landing gear came up right away and the airplanes never got above a hundred feet. In a loose trail, they *swung around to the left and came right at us. I've seen buzz-jobs – done more than a few myself – but this was the buzz-job to end all buzz-jobs. They were crazy angry. If it wasn't for the vehicles and aircraft we had all moved close to, they would have taken our heads off. The prop blast was a gale that closed eyes and made us gasp. I'll swear I felt the heat from their exhausts. I know I smelled it.*

The shootdown ruined Johnson. Not officially. As far as I know, the sad affair was hushed up as one of those events which happen during a war. But he was never the same. His tour with the 361th ended soon after that mission. He didn't leave the group in disgrace, but he didn't leave with a great hurrah either. I made attempts after the war to get in touch, but he never answered my letters.

The lesson here, is the effect your emotions can have on what you see. He wanted an air kill so badly that he convinced himself that the Spitfires *were "bandits", despite two radio calls which should have made him hesitate. I also think it was plain unlucky for him. Johnson was a good fighter pilot. He was aggressive. You had to be. Killing the enemy was first. Everything else had a lower priority.*

Still, as I was to later learn myself, thinking you shot a friendly is the most horrible feeling in the world. Your stomach bottoms out. You're nauseous with guilt that you killed a man by mistake.

14

BOTTISHAM II

Katzenjammer

On the Twentieth of July, Bill Kemp got his first victory in the air and did so in style.

The 361st Group was supporting heavy bombers in an attack on Köthen, an industrial complex north of Leipzig, deep in Germany. The fighters of the *Reichsverteidigung,* the *Luftwaffe*'s home defense force marked with red and white or black and white bands on their fuselages, came up in force.

Kemp was flying a P-51B as an element leader. In the swirling fury of one of the many dogfights on that mission, he picked out an *Me109* he sent down in flames. Minutes later, he shot up a *Focke-Wulf 190*.

What made Kemp's success more remarkable was the Fourth Fighter Group was also part of the escort force. Politics did play a part in mission assignments, no matter what was said officially. From intelligence sources and experience, which type of attack the *Luftwaffe* was going to use against the bomber columns was easily guessed. From the rear, overhead and straight down, head on, from the left or right. Even as *Luftwaffe* tactics shifted, the threat sector could usually be figured out. Consequently, the more aggressive commanders would ask for their groups to be assigned to the escort position where *Luftwaffe* attacks were most likely. These were the men who had some influence at 8th Fighter Command Headquarters. Men with reputations who commanded fighter groups with high collective scores and noted aces. The process was self engendering. Successful groups were given the prime positions where they would score more, be more successful, rate better positions the next mission, and so on. The Fourth Fighter Group, lead by Colonel Don Blakeslee and the with "Hub" Zemke leading, always seemed to get the choice escort positions. They would be the ones to engage the enemy – and get kills – while the rest could only listen on the R/T and gnash their teeth.

However, not all the time, as Bill Kemp showed that day. Talent and a little bit of luck would always let skill come to the fore. Lieutenant Sherman Armsby, also with the 375th, got a triple kill the same day Kemp got his two.

The routine after landing at Bottisham was to go straight to the large room in the operations building where hours before they had briefed for the mission. The furniture had been rearranged to make it into a debriefing area with spaces for individual flights. It was the domain of Captain Houston, Sergeant Cruikshank and their assistants. Returning pilots were supposed to go immediately to debrief. Even stops at the latrine were discouraged, although after six plus hours in the air, it was a rare pilot who made it all the way to the ops building without a relief stop. Coffee, water and sometimes, Cokes, were available in the debriefing area.

Debriefs were the nitty-gritty of combat. The flying and fighting did not bother most pilots. Trying to retell in detail what had happened when and where did. When bullets were flying, remembering what time it was, was difficult if not impossible. Ben was good at it. Houston usually let Lieutenant Drew wait until last to fill in the boasts and maybe's with facts.

The formal debrief over, the pilots did not head for their quarters and a shower. While they were waving their hands trying to reconstruct the un-rebuildable, the squadron photographic section was rushing to process film the armorers had snatched from the small movie camera in the wing's leading edge as soon as the propeller had stopped. The lengths of film from every airplane which had fired its guns were spliced into one reel so they could be viewed as soon as possible.

The room two doors down from the briefing room was a far cry from a movie theater stateside. Seating was on folding chairs with latecomers standing against the walls. A sixteen millimeter projector churned noisily and provided the only light. Polite silence was not the rule. Catcalls and razzberries, yells to freeze a frame, or to go back were frequent. Loud, disparaging comments on a squadron mate's aim were normal and expected. Only rarely, were cheers for a good shot or a clean kill heard. Viewing gun-camera film was not for the thin-skinned.

The Kemp—Drew rivalry grew during these sessions. Neither would give the other an inch. The rest of the squadron loved it. They had a couple of winners with them now, and they got to share in the glory. It did not matter that rules for the private feud were tougher than anything the Eighth Air Force had.

The Eighth Air Force recognized the difficulty of attacking airfields in Europe. The *Luftwaffe* bases were always heavily defended. Therefore, full credit was given for airplanes destroyed on the ground. However, that credit was granted only if another pilot was a witness or the kill could be proven by gun camera film. This was another reason why the immediate film screening was so well attended.

Tradition gave credit toward Ace status only for enemy airplanes downed in the air.

Kemp and Drew had their own rules. Those rules were never specified, nor written. They were designed to make it as difficult as possible for either to get ahead. Although they each soon had one on the ground and one and two in the air, by their own standards, neither had any score… yet.

Looking for a story, a couple of GI reporters from *Stars & Stripes* newspaper arrived at Bottisham. *Katzenjammer Kids*? It was a natural. Who first used the phrase is unknown, but given the popularity of the comic strip and the antics of Billy and Ben, it was fitting. When interviewed, their squadron commander, Major Roswell Freedman, set the tone of later articles by saying, "Heck, all this squadron has to do is send Kemp and Drew out a couple of minutes ahead and, as sure as night follows day, those boys will scare up the *Luftwaffe*."

The first article was in the "Personality" section. The next time the *Katzenjammer Kids* went out together, their escapade made *Stars and Stripes* and *Yank* magazine. They were famous.

15

CAMBRIDGESHIRE

The Bottisham Four

Fame arrives in many forms. For a fighter pilot in Europe, the obvious was thrilling air combats, many enemy airplanes shot down. Ben Drew had his share of that sort of glory, but his part in an event which received national publicity and later world wide distribution was by accident... and because he was lazy.

July Twenty-sixth was a stand-down day for the 361st Fighter Group. The preceding days had been busy and most of the pilots and airmen welcomed the chance to get off the base and relax. Bottisham was a pleasant town. *The Swan, The Greyhound, The Carpenter's Arms* were all pubs that welcomed the Americans. The surrounding countryside was rolling and green with footpaths for a stroll. London was a train ride away; an easy trip for anyone with a twenty-four hour pass. The airbase emptied fast on stand-down days.

Ben stayed in bed late. He was in no hurry. He had all day.

Late in the morning, he was getting dressed to go to London. "Red" Rowlett and Frank Glankler were with him when Colonel Christian came in. Senior officers always had paperwork and various administrative duties to keep them on base a little longer, but why was he in their barracks? He surprised the little group when he told them they were flying that afternoon.

Colonel Christian smiled and said, "The photographic section of the US Army needs publicity shots of *Mustangs*. This group was chosen. And I've picked you. A *Fortress* has been laid on as camera ship. The photographers will shoot from the waist stations. This is a big deal. They are shooting color as well as the usual stuff. I want us to look good. Briefing is at 1300." His smile broadened. "I want to thank you all for volunteering."

The result is probably the most widely seen photograph of airplanes in flight ever taken. The Army Air Force gave it wide distribution. In 1944, the picture, in color, was printed in many magazines. Boys all over America tacked or taped the picture to their walls. Years later, historians and model builders would argue about the picture. Nor was it the only photo. Each P-51 pulled alongside the *Fortress* for individual portraits. Black and white, they are exceptionally sharp and provide a definitive look at the airplanes of a fighting squadron at the height of the air war over Europe.

The Bottisham Four

The formation is all the more interesting because there are three different models of *Mustang* in it and each aircraft is unique with a story.

All carry the squadron code letters for the 375th Fighter Squadron: E2. In the phonetic alphabet of the time, E2 was spoken as "Easy Two." The third code letter individualized the airplanes. "Easy Two Charlie", "Sugar", "Able" and "How" make up the formation. The black and white stripes were added to assist recognition during the Normandy Invasion the month before. Orders to paint them on came late at night on the Fifth of June. The hard working enlisted airmen had less than six hours to do the job in the dark.

The Group Commanding Officer, Colonel Thomas J.J. Christian is leading in "Lou IV", E2*C. The first "Lou" was a P-47B *Thunderbolt* he flew when the group first came to England. It had a cartoon baby painted on its olive-drab nose. *Lou's* II and III were P-51B's. They were named after his infant daughter. Group, squadron and flight leaders rated the initial of their last name as the third letter. Hence, the C in "Easy Two Charlie" stands for Christian. His airplane is an early model P-51D without the swept fin from the fuselage to the tail. His is the only one with the group's new paint scheme which was yellow from the spinner all the way back to the firewall. "Lou IV" was shot down strafing a railway marshaling yard in France.

Ben Drew is in the unnamed "Easy Two Sugar"–the newest airplane in the photograph. E2*S is a P-51D with the small fin added to aid stability at high speed. The pilots called it a "B-17 fin" because of its shape. E2*S was assigned to a pilot named Rosenberger. Bill Kemp was flying E2*S on the crazy day at Chartres when he and Drew engaged forty German fighters. Days after that mission, a new replacement on a training flight spun into a cloud and crashed to end the career of "Easy Two Sugar".

"Sky Bouncer", E2*A, is a P-51D identical with Colonel Christian's "Lou IV" except for the rear view mirror on the canopy bow. Captain

Bruce Rowlett was the 375th Squadron's operation officer when he was "volunteered" for the photo flight. Rowlett's nickname was "Red" for the color of his hair. Four days earlier, had used "Sky Bouncer" to shoot down two *Me109s*.

"Suzy G", E2*H, is a P-51B, the oldest airplane in the formation. It was the personal ship of Frank Glankler, leader of D Flight before Bill Kemp. He had named the airplane after his wife. "Suzy G" was Drew's mount for his one-on-one dogfight near Rostock.

Glankler did two tours in the 361st. While he was home on leave between those tours in September, another pilot flew "Suzy G" on an escort mission to Magdeburg, was shot up, managed to return to England, but crashed in a field. The *Mustang's* back was broken and never flew again. Captain Glankler was given a brand new P-51D when he returned which he named the "Suzy G II".

The controversy the photograph caused was over the color of the upper fuselage and wings. Although the group's veterans who talked with the author said the airplanes were painted with standard, US Army issue, matte, olive-drab paint, many people believe the 361st painted their *Mustangs* blue. One possible explanation is the type of color film used, especially for reproductions, and the reflected sky give the dark upper surfaces a decidedly blue shade in most prints. Another possibility is that some, but not all, of the P-51s were indeed painted blue.

The 361st Fighter Group wisely did not depend on rank alone for leadership positions. Colonel Christian had started the policy. As he promised Kemp and Drew on their first day at Bottisham, if they were as good as their reputations, they would become flight leaders. They were. Both had two victories to their credit within their first month in combat.

Ben Drew flew his first mission as A flight leader on the 29th of July. He was still a second lieutenant. He had flown a half dozen flights as a wingman before becoming an element leader. When Martin Johnson left, his deputy took over for a quick ten days before he too rotated home and Ben was given A Flight.

Within days, Bill Kemp was made commander of D Flight when Frank Glankler went home on leave after completing his first tour. Interestingly, Glankler returned to the 375th as a Captain in late September and took over Ben's A Flight while Kemp on his second tour continued as leader of D Flight.

16

GERMANY

Horrido

From overhead the bomber formation looked solid. B-17 wings are broad and wide. Wings overlapped wings. Snowy contrails flowed out from every engine and swelled into whitely opaque streams as solid as rapids. The mass of airplanes flew close to each other. Close for protection. Protection from above and below. Protection in depth. Literal depth. From top to bottom the bomber formation was two thousand feet deep. And four miles long.

The *Messerschmitts* were faster than the formation. They flew over the bombers, out of gun range. The German fighters banked from side to side. Their pilots looking for gaps in the solidity, planning their attack. Setting in their minds the way the American formation would look when their gaggle had completed its maneuver and the attack began. How it would look when the shooting started and the view would be much different.

With their greater speed the *Luftwaffe* fighters rapidly pulled ahead. Banking occasionally to judge the distance – heads craned over shoulders to check the victims – the *Gruppe Kommandeur*, the *Staffel Käpitains*, calculated how far to fly. How far for a perfect attack. How far before it was time.

When it was time, the sleek fuselaged fighters with heavy cannon in their noses, began to roll. *Der Kommandeur* first, his new, and terrified, wingman and the *Stab* flight following. Then the *Käpitains* took their *staffels* over onto their backs. Thirty-six fighters rolled till the world was up and the sky was down.

The pilots pushed sticks to the side and booted rudders, watching the horizon spin crazily. As wings came past vertical, each pilot began to pull. Lazily at first, floating in their harnesses as the arc of flight canceled the pull of the earth. Then harder to save altitude. The Earth sought revenge – pulling on wing spars and engines, on flesh and muscle. Heads pulled back, necks strained, the pilots waited for the targets to appear in their gunsights as the split-ess maneuver pointed them at the bombers. Pointed them nose to nose with plenty of airspeed.

From the front a B-17 becomes a pattern of circles. Four round engines. Four propeller arcs, gleaming silver. A fat fuselage tipped with a round plastic cone over the bombardier. A half round navigator's bubble. A bigger half round on top that is the upper turret with twin fifty calibers. The ball turret dangling below with two more guns. And when in close, the round eye goggles of the pilots and gunners.

Lucky Thirteen. The American airmen named him that. He favored the number. Others thought thirteen bad luck. He did not. In his first *staffel* posting, 1/JG 51, at the end of the Battle of Britain, he was assigned an *Me109* with a large, white 13 on the fuselage. Partly, it was because the other pilots were superstitious; partly because it was the next airplane available for a new pilot.

Jagdgeschwader 51 was transferred to the East for Operation Barbarossa. On the first day of the invasion of the Soviet Union, he scored his first victories. Two of them. In the next month, he shot down ten more Russian airplanes. All while flying "White Thirteen". He was fearless.

A lucky *Flak* round brought him down in July of 1941 and he was sent to Germany to recover from his injuries. After that he was made the commanding officer of a squadron, a *staffel*, at the Zerbst fighter training school. It was an assignment that would affect the air war over Europe.

He was Georg-Peter Eder.

At Zerbst, Eder taught the latest *Luftwaffe* tactics and talked to the pilots who were flying against the increasing numbers of American daylight bombers. He chaffed at not flying in combat and finagled orders to *Jagdgeschwader* 2 as *Käpitain* of the Third *Staffel*. His Thirteen was now yellow. He was in the right place. The *Geschwader Kommodore* was Egon Mayer who had similar ideas on how to attack heavy bombers. The two of them are credited with developing the head-on attacks which the *Luftwaffe* would use successfully for the rest of the war.

Egon and Eder realized that the front of a bomber formation was the most weakly defended part. The first B-17s in Europe did not even have a nose turret. A nose-on attack also had the advantages of non-deflection shooting; the pilots did not have to judge "lead", and the high closure speed gave the bombers' gunners less time to defend themselves. However, the high closure speed was also a disadvantage. It gave the fighter pilots a very short time to aim and fire. The bombers flew at almost two hundred miles per hour, the fighters, after their dives, at over three hundred. The *Messerschmitt's* guns became effective at five hundred yards. That meant less than two seconds. A short time indeed.

The *Luftwaffe* pilots who were successful became expert at aiming fast.

Georg-Peter Eder was successful. He became a specialist in shooting down heavy bombers, B-17 *Flying Fortresses*, B-24 *Liberators*. When it was all over, Eder had shot down more *viermots*, four engine airplanes, than any man in history.

Eder using the fighter pilot's favorite training aid—his hands. In background is Me109G.

There were other types of attacks and variations on the straight nose-on assault to account for different aircraft and weapons. In an Eighth Air Force study done in late 1943, the intelligence specialists used the colorfully descriptive names the airmen themselves used: Rocketeers, Triple Threat, Tail Gunners' Headache, Roller Coaster, Pepper Spray, The Sister Act, Swooper, and The Twin-Engined Tail Pecker.

The reason allied airmen referred to Eder's favored number thirteen as "lucky" was the similar tales which made their way back to England. Surviving crewmen reported being shot up by a *Messerschmitt* with the number 13 on its side, which pulled away to allow them time to bail out.

Number 13 *Messerschmitt* would then blast what was left of their bomber out of the sky. Not many crewmen made it back from Europe so the legend took time to grow, but was eventually heard throughout the bomber wings of the Eighth Air Force. "Lucky Thirteen." You were lucky if it was Eder, although they did not know his name. Eder, the most chivalrous flier in an air war that had forgotten chivalry.

Back in the final months of 1940, some desk bound officer at the *Luftwaffe* high command, *OKL*, decreed that the traditional markings on fighters which identified leaders, experienced pilots and high scorers must be eliminated. It was probably the most ignored *Luftwaffe* regulation of all time. Asking high spirited and proud fighter pilots to remove their badges was like asking a medieval knight to paint his shield grey.

Geschwader and *Gruppe* commanders were to remove the double chevrons from fuselage sides. There would be no more victory bars painted on rudders. *Staffel* leaders were told not to fly in airplane number one as they had before.

The regulation worked in Eder's favor. As a *staffel käpitain* he could keep his lucky thirteen... and claim he was following regulations by doing so.

The sixteen *Me109s* of *Staffel 12/JG2*, followed Eder in "Blue 13" through the split-ess and drew apart. Each pilot picked a distant dot that would soon be a B-17. As the range closed each made small adjustments to put the gunsight pipper in the exact center of a circle. Glowing tracers floated from the bombers and dropped as nervous gunners fired before the attackers were in range.

Eder used thumb and forefinger to fire both his machine guns and cannon when he was in sure range. At the last instant, he rolled his fighter and dived beneath the giant bomber. He kept rolling until upright and immediately sought out another bomber. Shoot and roll.

Shoot and roll. Then there were no more targets in front of him. He laid his *Messerschmitt* on its side and pulled hard back towards the formation. He was looking for the bombers he had shot. Looking for bombers his men had shot. Looking for the *Herausschutzen*. The bombers which had been knocked out of the formation. The culls, the wounded airplanes. The doomed airplanes.

Horrido had emotional meaning to *Luftwaffe* pilots far beyond the cry's derivation. Saint Horridus is the patron saint of hunters. The victory yell when prey fell during the hunt, was "*Horrido, horrido!*" The hunters of the sky had taken the call aloft. As "Tallyho" came to mean more than "I see the enemy", so did "*Horrido*" signify more than "I have hit my target." *Horrido* became an exultant call of identity – "I am a fighter pilot. I am victorious."

Leutnant Georg-Peter Eder with *staffel* mascot *Schnauser* at the tail of his Messerschmitt 109.

The attack had been a good one. "*Horrido*" had crackled over the radio many times. One *Flying Fortress* was a clean kill. It had spun down a mass of flame. Two others had streams of black smoke and were descending, slowing. Eder counted three more trails of black smoke from bombers which had managed to stay in formation... for a while. Another trail was white; probably high octane aviation gasoline. He headed for the descending bomber on the left. He checked his ammunition counters. There were bullets and shells enough for more work. It was time for the *coup de grace.*

The destruction of bombers was important to the *Luftwaffe*. In order to reward the pilots who attacked these difficult and dangerous targets a scoring system was implemented. The credits gained were used to determine awards and promotions. The maximum was four credits for the complete destruction of a four engined heavy bomber. Medium bombers were worth two points and two points were also given for damaging a heavy *viermot* enough to drive it out of the formation. Pilots scoring on the final destruction of a cull got one credit – the same as a pilot who knocked down a single-engined fighter – no matter how difficult the preceding dogfight had been. The destruction of bombers had the highest priority.

Eder became an expert in the destruction of heavy bombers. The *Luftwaffe* did not recognize the title of "ace". In the First World War a pilot with ten victories was called a "*Kanone*". The custom did not carry over. Instead, during 1939-1945, the *Luftwaffe* had *experten*. The word translates as it sounds; experts. For fighter pilots there was no set number of kills. For bomber pilots, no minimum number of missions. There were transport pilots who were considered *experten*. The qualification was as much for sustained performance, teaching ability and leadership as it was for specific achievement. Eder was an *expert*.

Eder's last kill of the day was an easy one. There were no Allied fighters around to worry about. A young sergeant pilot of his *staffel* was off to his right. Eder accelerated alongside the crippled Fortress looking it over. He saw no one in the windows of the tailgun enclosure under the rudder. The guns of the belly turret pointed straight down. He pulled up and barrel-rolled behind the bomber. His impromptu wingman followed. He put his pipper on the empty tail gunners window and shot a burst of cannon up the length of the fuselage. Nudging rudder and banking slightly, Eder slid behind the number two engine and fired again. He heard three thumps from his cannon and it stopped. Seconds later so did his two MG131 machine guns. The engine smoked and stopped. He waved the *Feldwebel* over and pulled clear to watch. The new man put a burst into the right outboard engine which burst into flames. The B-17's nose came up and the left wing fell. The bomber went into a spin. *Horrido!*

The debrief on who did what would be a mess. It usually was after a mission like this. However, there would be more missions; more bombers. In the long run, credit would go where credit was due.

17

ALPS

Postcard

A mission can stand out in a pilot's memories for many reasons. Even in the midst of war, death and destruction are not always involved. On the first day of August, Ben Drew flew one of his most memorable missions. There was no combat. No one was hurt. There were no deeds of daring-do. In fact, the *Luftwaffe* was never seen.

The job of the 361st Fighter Group that day was to escort Eighth Air Force bombers far down into southern France. So far down, that straying across the Franco-Swiss border was a worry. The bomber's mission was to drop, not bombs, but supplies to the French Resistance, the FFI.

Not knowing what was to come, Ben figured the mission would be a long one; a six hour round-trip. But when he got to the target area, time became too short and he wished he had more.

Anti-aircraft fire, *Flak*, had dwindled as the group flew south until there was none. The sky was clear and clean. As the pilots said, you could see all the way to tomorrow.

In the far distance, fragments of white coalesced out of the far horizon. The fragments confused the eye. At first, they looked like distant clouds. As the distance closed, the white was too well defined to be cloud. The tops were hard edged and jagged; the bottoms well defined and bordered with grey stone. The horizon became steep and craggy. It was not sky. It was rock. Solid and impressive. The pilots were seeing the Alps. For youngsters from the flat plains of the Midwest or the eastern states with the old, smooth Appalachians, the Alps were the highest, the roughest, the most awesome peaks they had seen. They did not have to look up. The peaks were at their altitude, 15,000 feet high. The pilots could look with their eyes level. As they flew closer, the snow topped peaks replaced the horizon.

The starkness of the topmost levels, melted fast into green slopes. Grass and trees. White among the greenery were tiny splashes of streams running downhill over rocks into rapids. Closer still, and picture perfect villages were visible. Peaked homes and inns, gentle roads, fences around pastures, farm fields dotted the deep valleys. Images from a fairy tale – or a post card

The fighter pilots were used to watching as rows of dark bombs rushed from open bomb bays. Always from up high, above 20,000 feet. This time, the bomber leader took the massive formation down to 3,000 feet over the foothills. Cloth panels had been spread on the ground to mark the aim points. Oversize table cloths for a picnic.

None of the pilots had been on a mission like this before. They did not know what to expect. The bomb doors came open as usual as the heavies flew straight and level. Dark objects tumbled down, fell for a few seconds until the parachutes streamed and opened. The scene was from *Fantasia*, from The *Wizard of Oz*. Like so many flower petals or butterflies, the canopies in bright colors floated and danced.

In reality the parachutes were in different colors so the partisans could tell what type of materiel was suspended from which parachute. But the wads of silk tumbling from bomb bays were not reality. Red and blue and green and white and orange, they were blossoms in an aerial bouquet, floating earthward to lie spread in the green fields below. Seen from the air, the groups of resistance men could have been gnomes scurrying to gather scattered treasures and hide them in secret places.

The scene was enchanting, unreal.

The flight went up a valley with the snowy peaks high around the silver airplanes. The red roofs of farmhouses and the narrow, twisty streets of villages passed below spinning propellers. The rainbow of parachutes far behind in their wake.

Far ahead, a distinctive, pure white triangle reached over the lesser peaks, Mount Blanc. Her summit obvious against the solid blue sky.

A lone British *Mosquito* was with the task force as a weather observer and streaked down the valley, flying just above the tree tops. The pilot and his observer indulging in the glorious moments granted only to airmen at one with their machine in beautiful terrain. They hopped over ridges and down rills, over crests and into shadowed valleys. The higher flying fighter and bomber crews that spotted the low flyer were envious.

Normally, the turn toward home after the bomb run was eagerly awaited, sought after. Over the softly rolling country of southernmost France, with the sky clear and no enemy near, the airmen treated the time to go back in the same way a child delays bedtime. Every man wished that he might remain suspended there in space over the peaceful countryside. For the moment, the war was very far away. Ben thought how wonderful it would be to return someday when peace was a reality and not an illusion and visit the green, peaceful land below. He later traveled the world, but never did return to the Alpine peaks and meadows.

18

CHARTRES

No Ammo

Drew log book: escort Bordeaux/Chartres, Aug 8 '44. Claimed damaged three trucks (the French car) and flak towers and damage to 109. Kemp claimed 190 and damage to 109.

Extract from Mission Summary Report: 375th Fighter Squadron, 7 August, 1944
1 FW190 DESTROYED   LT. KEMP   (AIR)
1 FW190 DAMAGED   LT. DREW   (AIR)
1 FW190 DAMAGED   LT. KEMP   (AIR)
1 ME109 DAMAGED   LTS. KEMP & WOOD (GND)

Ben Drew had screwed up... again. Nothing major. He had buzzed the field. Unfortunately, Major Cummins who was now the group operations officer was watching. He was not impressed by these two hot-shot lieutenants. They had been made flight leaders and they each had scored against the *Luftwaffe*, but he believed in the "book" and Drew needed disciplining. For the next escort mission he assigned Ben as Kemp's wingman. He knew Drew would hate that more than anything.

No one knew who first began to refer to them as the *Katzenjammer Kids*, but it was appropriate. They were boisterous, eager for a fight, and always on the fringes of trouble. If Major Cummins could have known what the one mission the *Katzenjammer Kids* flew together would turn into, he would not have chosen such a punishment for Ben Drew.

I am so ashamed of that mission. I've thought about it all these years. Kemp and I were both flight commanders, but I'd buzzed the field, or something fun like I did a lot, and this stiff-neck major we had in the outfit made me fly on Kemp's wing. He knew how I would hate that. I was used to leading my own flight.

So I went out as Kemp's number three and there was nothing going on. We had both found a way to get away from the bombers and go looking for targets of opportunity. Kemp starts easing away from the squadron. He's nearly out of sight. He calls on the radio, "Hey leader, I've got bogies, three o'clock low. Permission to go" And since it was so quiet, he got a clearance to go. There were no bogies. There wasn't an enemy airplane for miles around. We just wanted to find something to shoot at.

We're down low, weaving over the countryside and here comes this civilian automobile. I'm a little ashamed of myself to this day, but we were told that the French knew whenever our airplanes were overhead, not to move, don't budge, because we'd shoot at anything that did move. The reasoning was that anyone driving a car had to be German, or a German sympathizer. So here comes this little deuce rolling on down the highway. Well, we hadn't found anything else worth shooting at, so I said, "Billy, I got a target."

Kemp and Leonard Wood, the number two man, stay high and watch as I head down and put about a hundred rounds into this car. It slithers off to the side, but doesn't burn. I come around again and put about 400 more bullets into the wreck. If there was anything at all in the car it was totally destroyed. But what a waste. That little French car wasn't worth ten rounds, much less what I shot at it.

Billy calls me off, "OK, that's enough of this fun for a while. Let's go look around."

We find some Flak *towers and the three of us shoot at them. A pointless waste.* Flak *towers were made of heavy concrete with very narrow slits for the guns. We just wanted to shoot at something. All our bullets did was make puffs of dust where they hit the concrete.*

We stay low, generally heading for the Channel and home. All of a sudden, we are in the middle of the traffic pattern at Chartres. Heck, I wasn't really paying attention – Kemp was leading, not me. There are at least fifty Luftwaffe *fighters all around us. A mix of 109s and 190s, taking off, getting into formation.*

Kemp says, "Bingo, bingo! Drew, we got 'em"'

As we waded into the Jerries, *I thought, talk about an ace in a day.*

They could easily have avoided the *Luftwaffe* airfield. The swarm of airplanes would have been visible from miles away. A change of direction would have taken their small flight well out of the way. They all were keen-eyed and on the lookout for targets. They were all also cocky and aggressive.

Surprise and numbers were both on the Americans' side. The three *Mustangs* were the middle of the formation before the Germans realized they were there and it took more moments for them to react. With over ten Germans for every Yank, they got in each other's way. Normal battle order was not yet formed. Wingmen looked for flight leaders. Leaders maneuvered to get a shot. They all tried to avoid colliding with each other. It was chaos in a small space. The highest airplanes were at 1,500 feet when the brawl began.

Kemp was first in. He had an easy shot at a Focke-Wulf 190 which had just retracted its wheels. He got hits, but Wood called a break because of a closing Me109. Out of his hard turn, Kemp found himself close to another FW190. He fired from twenty-five yards and the German exploded in a fireball which tumbled to the ground 300 feet below.

Second Lieutenant Wood was flinging his Mustang around trying to cover Kemp's tail while doing some shooting of his own. He was on his first close encounter with enemy aircraft. All three of them were talking rapidly on the radio. The squadron was in the air and trying to find out where the trio was. Wood's quick description of the cathedral told them.

Pilots still on the ground were jumping out of their aircraft. A Me109 tore through electric wires and ground looped in a rush to land. Kemp and Wood strafed it in a grass field. As the flew over the wrecked fighter, Kemp called, "Dammit. I'm out of ammo."

The Focke-Wulf and Messerschmitts were swinging their noses back in, trying to line up their gunsights.

Ben had picked out a Focke-Wulf which could not see him. It was an easy shot from six o'clock. Half his guns stuttered briefly. He was also out of ammunition. He told Kemp.

The *Focke-Wulf* pilot was not stupid. He realized an American fighter was directly behind him and not shooting. There could only be one reason. He toggled off the fuel tank on his belly. The big sixty-six gallon tank came straight at Ben's windscreen. He yanked back on his stick and flew three feet over it.

The *Focke-Wulf* reefed around and fired a long burst. Another *FW190* was shooting at his right side. Ben dived for the deck and jinked hard. He looked frantically for Kemp and Wood. He saw a silver airplane surrounded by a dozen green ones. He pulled up to go over a building.

Four *Messerschmitts* behind Wood sprayed cannon and machine-gun fire, but none could shoot accurately because of the others. Wood pushed on his throttle to go into combat boost. The lever would not move. It was already as far forward as it would go. Had been for some time. He saw Kemp in Easy Two Sugar ahead to his left. A pair of 190s flew across his nose heading for Kemp. He fired at them without aiming.

Kemp saw the fighters on his right, but knew they were too late. They slid behind him. He looked in his mirrors and saw he was pulling away from the pack behind him. He had made it. They all had.

We had each been in combat boost a long time. Sucked a lot more gas than we figured on. We eventually felt safe enough to slow down and get joined up again, but we had to land at Manston for fuel. My airplane, E2*N, had busted a magneto at some point. I said the hell with it and took it back to Bottisham without waiting to get it fixed.

As soon as we landed, Billy telephoned the 361st and told them about all the *Luftwaffe* fighters back at Chartres. They had figured out where we were and decided to land and top off with fuel. I was impressed. By the time we got back to Bottisham, most of the wing had gotten back in the air. They didn't find anything when they got to Chartres, but they sure made a good try.

I still wonder. If it hadn't been for that one little French car, I might have had ten airplanes. Ten.

Lieutenants Ben Drew, Bill Kemp and Leonard Wood in a publicity shot after the dogfight over the *Luftwaffe* aerodrome at Chartres. The airplane may be the P-51B which Drew was flying, E2*N.

Colonel Christian, Commanding Officer of
361st Fighter Group from its beginning.

19

THE ENGLISH CHANNEL

Dull Duty

CALLSIGNS: *Cadet* = 375th Fighter Squadron, *Globeright* = 361st Fighter Group, *Colgate* = English radar station which relayed calls to the bases inland, *Lakepress* = Bottisham air base.

15,000 feet below, the English Channel was glittery blue. Occasional whitecaps ruffled the surface and gave texture to the water. The *Merlin* ran smoothly and Ben's oxygen mask hung off to one side. He was alone. No formation to hold position in. No eternal neck twisting to spot *Luftwaffe* fighters. Radio relay was easy duty. It was to be one of the worst days of his life.

During missions over the continent, each fighter group would position one of their aircraft over The Channel to relay radio reports back to their home base. It was Ben's turn to relay for the 361st back to Bottisham. He chaffed at missing the chance to do some shooting, but it was better than sitting on the ground. The flying was easy and every so often, there were impromptu dog fights with other relay ships or RAF and USAAF fighters on engine tests.

Colonel Christian was leading all the squadrons that day. I can't tell you enough what a great leader he was. A true gentleman. He was the first

West Pointer to command a fighter wing in the Eighth Air Force. He had certainly made me feel important from the first time I walked into his office.

He had something of an odd background. Before the war, he was a bomber pilot. A four engine bomber pilot. Shows you how strange things got after Pearl Harbor. Experienced pilots were in demand.

Christian had formed the 361st Fighter Group back in Richmond, Virginia and taken it to England while the group was flying "Jugs", P-47s. The 361st had arrived at Bottisham the very end of 1943 and flown their first missions in January of '44, so he had been there a while. There were still a handful of the "old gang" there when I arrived. Marty Johnson who lead me on my first trips. Cole who was also a good navigator. Joe Kruzel who later lead the group. Glankler who did two tours of duty. Their experience was invaluable.

Before I became leader of A flight, I flew a handful of missions as Christian's wingman. Flew a couple after that too. He had asked me. Odd conversation.

We were talking in the officers' club about a week after I had arrived. He wasn't stuffy about rank despite being from the Point. Among other things, I learned he was the great grandson of "Stonewall" Jackson. He said, "Drew, I hear that you've got good eyes."

I admitted I saw 'em as soon as anyone.

He said, "Good. I want you to fly on my wing. I can't see worth a damn and I want you to be my eyes. You call 'em out, and I'll take it from there."

I was kind of shocked. I mean, as fighter jocks we were all proud of how far away we could pick up bogies and tell what they were. Here was my wing commander admitting to me, a mere lieutenant, that he couldn't see. It wasn't that his vision was bad, it just wasn't sharp enough for the edge you needed in combat. But that was the kind of man he was. He could admit his own failings. A superb leader.

He had named his airplanes "Lou" after his daughter. He had never seen the little girl. His wife was expecting when he left for England. The first Lou *was a P-47. By the time I joined the 375th squadron, at his behest remember, he was on his third P-51, a D model, an early one without the fillet forward of the vertical fin. That ship was* Lou IV, *immortalized by an Eighth Air Force photographer the end of July.*

"Colgate, this is Cadet Two, Colgate, this is Cadet Two for relay to Lakepress. How do you read me? Over."

Ben waited ten seconds before answering. "Cadet Two, this is Colgate relay. Go ahead."

"Roger relay. Pass to base, the Colonel is down. I repeat, the Colonel is down."

Stunned, Ben did not answer, then realized he had to or Cadet Two would broadcast again. "Roger, Two, copy your message." It took more minutes before he could bring himself to tell Bottisham that the leader of the 361st had been killed.

After escorting a formation of B-17s to Bonville, Colonel Christian had lead the wing down in a bombing attack against rail transport targets; yards, rolling stock, locomotives. His wingman that day was 2Lt Robert Bain of 376th Squadron. Much later, it was learned that Lou IV had crashed near the village of Boisleaux-au-Mont.

Wingman's statement from Colonel Christian's IDPF (Individual Deceased Personnel File.):

"I was flying position number 3 of a 3 ship flight led by Col. Christian. We approached the railroad marshalling yards at Arras, France, from the northeast direction at an altitude of 11,000 feet. We circled the target receiving instructions from Col. Christian to make the bomb run from south to east, pulling up to the left after bombing. We were in a string formation, my postion number 2 trailing our leader. The Colonel executed a half roll and Split S from 11,000 feet. I watched his descent until about 6,000 feet, and then made my dive at 3,000 feet. I banked left,and climbed to 6,000 feet and looked for the leader. Number 3 ship pulled up near me, but neither he nor I could [see] Col. Christian. I observed a very good hit in the center of the rail yards, not caused by number 3 man or myself, and assumed it was the Colonel's bombs. I repeatedly called our leader over the radio, but never received an answer. The attack took place at 1505, 12 August. 1944.

Subscribed and sworn to by 2Lt. Robert J. Bain, 376th Squadron."

Colonel Christian was not the group's only loss.

"Colgate relay, this is Cadet Two, pass to base, Rainey is down. Rainey. Good chute reported. Over."

Then, too few minutes later, "Colgate relay, this is Cadet Two, pass to base, Engstrom is down. Wingman saw him on the ground. Engstrom. You copy?"

August Twelfth had to be one of the grimmest days of my life. There I sat, fat, dumb and happy over the Channel, and I had to relay all the bad news back to base.

Amazingly, both Rainey and Engstrom, evaded the Germans and local sympathizers and made it back to England. They met each other soon after in a London hotel that was a clearing center. A pilot named Zieske had also bailed out, but witnesses said that his chute didn't open and he was killed. But it was Christian going down that hit me – hell, hit all of us – the worst. He had made the 361st the great outfit that it was. We tracked all the reports, but nothing definite came in. What happened to his mortal remains was a mystery for many years.

20

WITMUND

The Bleeder

I remember the August 15 mission to Witmund for two reasons. Billy Kemp almost bought it and I saw one of the bravest men ever.

We were strafing a night fighter aerodrome in Germany. I had a section of eight airplanes on the left. Kemp had eight on the right. Sixteen Mustangs line abreast.

Even moving fast, down low, some details are frozen in memory. Down at fifty feet, 300 knots, I noticed this German gunner. Noticed him because he was standing up. Standing up and stripped to the waist.

There were revetments all over the field; beyond the runways. This crazy man had a machine gun and was standing on the pile of earth surrounding a revetment, facing down sixteen Mustangs. *He was firing from his hip. Not aiming, blazing away like mad. Swinging the muzzle side to side at us.*

He was between me and the Mustang *on my right so I couldn't turn to shoot at him. I had my trigger down, but don't know where my bullets were going because I wasn't aiming. I was fascinated with this* Jerry *standing, all alone, completely exposed, shooting at us. I was watching him instead of my gunsight. I got a close look as I flew by. He had swung the blazing gun at me. His face was set with concentration. He aimed the best he could with the heavy gun down on his hip. I thought, "When it comes to bravery this guy is A-number-one. Taking on sixteen* Mustangs *each with six fifty caliber guns."*

I assume he survived our attack. He was in a great position lined up between two of us. Neither of us could bring his guns to bear. A strafing run in squadron strength was like that. Not a whole lot of room to move. By then we'd pretty much given up making multiple passes. Once the gunners were alerted, they were tough. No sense in giving them a second crack at you. We lost far too many airplanes during low level attacks. It was probably the most dangerous thing we had to do. That is why the Eighth Air Force gave full credit for aircraft destroyed on the ground. It was hard. And men like that Kraut *gunner were the reason. Truly a brave man. I happened to notice this one, but there were a lot more like him out there.*

I was still thinking about him as I moved my pipper onto a hangar.

Over the radio I heard Kemp call, "I'm hit. I'm hit."

I got on the radio before Globe Right, *the group commander, did and asked,* "Black Leader, *how bad are you hit?"*

"I don't know, but I'm bleeding. My ship seems OK."

This scared me because I was one of the few people who knew that Bill Kemp was a hemophiliac, a bleeder. It sounds wild that he could have made it into the Army Air Forces, but I guess back then, it was not one of the things they checked on. Even crazier was that he had made it through all those Golden Gloves Boxing tournaments without being found out. It's a testament to just how good he was. No fighter managed to hit him hard enough to start him bleeding. But now, with him alone in the cockpit of a fighter over Germany, I was worried.

I asked if he wanted one or two of our guys to escort him back. He said, "No, no. I'll be better off by myself."

He was a flight leader and what he said went, so we let him climb away alone.

Kemp's airplane was a P-51D with large, black E2*X on the sides. It had the yellow nose of all the 361 Group's airplanes. He had named it

"Betty Lee" after his wife. The name was painted in flowing red letters. In smaller lettering underneath, the assistant crew chief, Sergeant Bernard Redden, had added his girlfriend, "Marie". Dual names were a common practice and the chances were the crew chief's sweetheart's name would last longer as the airplane was "his" with the pilots only borrowing it for their tour.

A box of B-24 *Liberators* was on its way back to home base in England. The *Liberators* were a mix of older, olive drab painted machines with a scattering of shiny, new, aluminum B-24Js. For some reason the formation was unescorted. There were no friendly fighters anywhere near. While it was not uncommon, it was definitely not smart.

Kemp saw the formation and figured out from its heading and location that it was returning to England. He pushed the *Betty Lee's* throttle forward and climbed to join them.

A good fighter pilot never stops scanning the sky. As Kemp came closer to the bombers, he saw that the sky was not empty of fighters. There was a large formation of *Luftwaffe Me109s* positioning for an attack on the *Liberators*. As he watched, the Germans pushed over into an attack dive.

Bleeding or not, Bill Kemp never hesitated. He re-checked that his gun switches and gunsight were on. He pointed the yellow nose of his *Mustang* straight into the pack of thirty *Messerschmitts*. The range decreased rapidly. He made small adjustments of stick and rudder to put his pipper on the lead *Me109*. When in range, he squeezed the trigger. Seven months of constant gunnery practice were behind his aim. The *Luftwaffe* pilot had not fired his cannon. Was he looking only at his intended victims, the lumbering bombers? He could have fired first and out-ranged Kemp – if he had thought of it. Instead, the slugs from *Betty Lee's* six machine guns reached out first.

Thirty enemy fighters flashed past as Kemp pulled the P-51 up hard in a high-side reversal. He had to chase them down before they could get at the bombers. Nose down, throttle past the emergency gate, he looked for targets.

There were none.

Only the tight formation of bombers was in front of him. Turrets and guns swiveling.

Kemp banked one way, then the other. Looking. All the 109s had turned tail and were retreating east. Was his attack that much of a surprise? Did the Germans think he was part of a large flight? It made no difference. The bombers were safe.

Kemp reduced power and let his airspeed slow. As he came near the bombers with their itchy gunners, he flew parallel outside of gun range so they could get a good look at who he was. This was no time for mistaken identities. The last part of the rendezvous was slow.

The co-pilot in the *Liberator* on the right of the formation waved as Kemp closed. So did the waist gunner. The upper turret had pointed his guns away and watched the approach over his shoulder. They may not have been there had Kemp not arrived when he did. Or had the courage to go after the Germans alone.

When the broad estuary of The Wash came in view. Kemp waggled his wings in farewell, and headed for his base at Bottisham.

He had called ahead and the crash trucks and ambulances were parked alongside the runway, red lights winking.

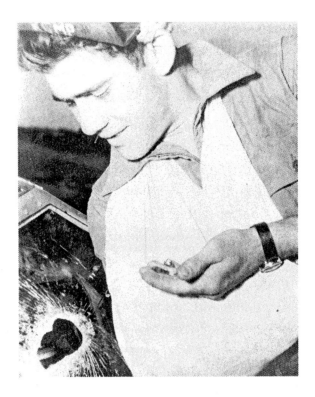

Bill Kemp admiring the hole in his windscreen after he was hit strafing. He holds the shrapnel that was removed from his arm which is still in a sling.

The landing was feather soft with his usual delicate touch. Rollout was straight down the center of the runway. The trucks swung out and drove after *Betty Lee* as the P-51 rolled past. They reached a good clip for Kemp's airplane did not slow down much. Somehow Kemp got the Mustang into her revetment where it spun around with one wheel brake locked. His maintenance crew got the airplane stopped and the semi-conscious Kemp out of the cockpit. *Betty Lee* was home.

After seeing *Betty Lee*, Sergeant Davis described the cockpit to Drew as, "More blood than I ever saw while slaughtering pigs back in Minnesota."

Four days later, Ben was asked if he would like to visit Kemp in the hospital. He jumped at the chance. It was a short visit; they were trying to get Kemp healthy enough to travel to London. With the enthusiastic endorsement of an entire B-24 squadron, a Distinguished Service Cross for this pilot who "single handed fought off thirty attacking *Me109s*," had been speedily approved. General Spaatz himself was to present America's second highest award.

Humor among combat pilots is strange. The daily exposure to death plays a large part. Most are very young. Early maturity is forced over the exuberance of youth. The result is an insulating cynicism and jokes which strike the outsider as odd.

Kemp's wound was not seriously damaging. He could have gone home, but asked for, and was, put back on flight status within weeks. The German bullet had torn open the soft upper part of his arm. The risk had been from a loss of blood. The squadron flight surgeon, Doctor Maynard Emlaw, un-medically described his treatment as, "pumping gallons of blood into him."

Ben sat in a metal chair, leaned back on the rear legs with one foot on the white painted frame of the hospital bed. Kemp's right arm was bandaged and in a sling. The head section of the bed was tilted up.

"Damn, Billy, that's a hell of a way to get out of the war. Letting yourself get hit like that. I mean you've missed four missions already. If it wasn't you, I'd call you a coward."

Kemp glared. "Drew, I don't like your sense of humor."

Ben pressed on. "And I also know exactly what happened. Don't tell me you got out there and shot up a 109 just to save those B-24s. I know you better. You were bleedin' to death, you didn't think you could find England, so you crawled up to the 24s and tagged along for the ride."

Kemp sat up straight, grunting as his hurt arm moved. He shook his good fist at Ben. "So help me, when I get out of here, I'm gonna level you." Ben just grinned.

Ben was stretched out on his bunk when Kemp barged into his quarters. He had just gotten off the train from London. He had ridden all the way with the medal, not just the ribbon, pinned to his uniform blouse. He leaned over and tapped the gold cross with the eagle in the center, making it swing.

"Well, Drew," he said loudly, "that ain't so bad for hiding behind some *Liberators*, is it?"

They stayed friends and the *Katzenjammer Kids'* reputation grew.

21

ROSTOCK

One versus One

One versus one in combat is rare. It has been glamorized in the pulp magazines and by Hollywood, but in reality, it almost never happens. Two equal, or even similar, aircraft, flown by equal pilots will inevitably wind up in a turning contest with neither gaining the advantage. In a combat situation, no pilot dares stay in an extended turn for more than a minute – the likelihood of a third fighter coming in is too high. Most combat is flown slash and go. Tracking and firing lasts only heart beats before it is vital to break off and look for the enemy who is, or will be, shooting at you. Individual airplanes fighting one on one for more than moments is unlikely, unsafe and... difficult.

Ben Drew continued to be eager for combat. Now that he was "A" flight leader he would not have to depend as much on chance. He would now be the first to shoot while his wingman and second element protected him. On August 25, the squadron was scheduled for a "Ramrod", a bomber escort mission followed by free patrol, to Rostock on the Baltic coast.

Ben lead the four *Mustang*s of "A" Flight, callsign "White", off the ground and headed for join-up with the rest of the squadron and group. As he climbed, he started to swear. The *Merlin* engine's supercharger was not cutting in properly. The airplane would be worthless at high altitude.

"Cadet leader, this is White leader. I've got a bum engine. Heading back. White Three, you got the flight."

Taxiing back in, Ben saw the ready spare airplane and remembered that as a flight leader, he was allowed to take the squadron spare. He would have to hurry.

He parked next to the spare and hollered at the first mechanic who came up, "This one's supercharger doesn't work. I'm taking the spare." He unplugged his radio leads and disconnected his oxygen hose, unsnapped the parachute clasps at his thighs and on his chest. Shrugged out of the parachute. Carrying his maps in one hand; helmet, gloves and Mae West still on, he jogged over to the waiting P-51B, climbed onto the wing and into the cockpit. The crew chief was waiting and helped strap him in. The crew chief was climbing down from the wing when Ben yelled, "Clear!" and pressed the starter button.

The airplane was the *Suzy G*, E2*H. Normally Frank Glankler's ship. Frank had been leader of "D" flight before turning it over to Billy Kemp. Now he was home in the States, so his airplane was flown by other pilots. Ben remembered the *Suzy G* had been on the photo mission the day he didn't get off base fast enough. She was a veteran; one of the first *Mustangs* in the 375th.

Heading for the runway on the perimeter was another P-51. It was on the same radio frequency as Ben. A second *louie* from New York named Beder. He wasn't senior enough to rate a spare, so must have been delayed for maintenance. They decided to go together to try and catch the strike group. Ben led. It was good to have a wingman.

The impromptu element was near the target area when Ben spotted a flight of four P-38 *Lightnings* well above them and a long way off. They were on a converging course. Farther away, was a large formation of *Luftwaffe* fighters. Me 109s. Probably an entire *Geschwader*, thirty plus airplanes. Horrified, Ben watched as a dozen of them peeled off and headed for the *Lightnings*.

He called his wingman and asked if he had been briefed about any P-38's in the area. The answer was a negative.

The radios in fighter aircraft had four pre-set channels; A, B, C, and D. The settings varied from group to group depending on what mission they were on. What channels were used for what was part of the mission briefing. Ben had no way to contact the four *Lightnings*.

The Germans were good. In one pass they flamed one *Lightning* and sent two down with smoking engines.

The twelve plane *Staffel* pulled up and re-joined the formation. Ben had headed toward the P-38's in an attempt to assist and now found himself pointing at the German flight. Another twelve – or were they the same? – came down at him. He called his wingman, "We'll go straight at 'em. It'll be worse if we turn. Shoot straight and good luck."

The crossing was mayhem. Two silver airplanes among a flock of dark green ones. All turning. All looking for a shot.

After he cleared the *melee*, Ben kept his nose up for altitude and kicked back in a rudder turn. Coming the other way was the *staffel* leader. Neither had a shot. They passed close. Ben threw a quick scan around him. No airplanes in sight except the black nosed *Messerschmitt* rolling into a hard bank. Ben tightened his own turn as much as he dared without stalling out.

The *Luftwaffe* pilot did the same.

Both airplanes were racked over in vertical banks. One wing pointed at the sky. The other pointed at the ground. The two machines went round and round like metal toys in a giant cylinder. From above their paths were a circle. From the side a spiral. No matter how hard the pilots tried to stay level they were descending.

Ben reached up with his left hand – the throttle would stay full forward – and quickly tightened the straps of the mask on his face. Then reached down and selected the 100% oxygen setting – he would need every bit of breath he could draw. He knew that in the other cockpit, his enemy was doing the same.

Ben lost count of how many times they had gone around. The sharp edge of sun shadow flooding the cockpit interior marked the revolutions. The distant, hazy horizon was a reference, not a direction. He had to keep his nose within a degree of where it was. Higher or lower, the geometry would change.

An airplane does not have to go slow to stall. A high speed stall can come at any time. Turning equals load factor. The higher the load, the higher the stall speed. That was the equation they were fighting. Pull too hard and the wing would shudder, about to lose lift. Do not pull hard enough and the other airplane cuts the distance. It is a fine balance. Delicate to maintain despite the forces racking airframe and human body.

Ben was breathing hard. He was a good athlete and in shape, but the constant G was exhausting. His arms were heavy. His grip on the control stick difficult. The parachute harness, life preserver, flight suit, his sweat shirt all grew in weight and pressed on his chest. His chest weighed more and pressed on his lungs. It was hard to breath. His neck was the worst. To keep his enemy in sight, he had to hold his head twisted over his shoulder and tilted up. His head was heavy. Helmet, goggles, earphones added their weight. The damned mask pulled on his face, cut into the bridge of his nose.

Around and around. Points on twined circles. Unchanging distances.

They were getting lower. Positions on opposite sides of the circle unchanged. Ben cracked open his flaps. Airspeed dropped. Turn radius decreased. The German cracked his too. The spiral steepened. The flaps went back into the wings.

Ben worried that another fighter would show up. He would be easy to attack from outside the circle. The German pilot had the same worry. Both hoped if there was a third airplane that it would be one of their own. Neither dared to look around. Their total concentration was on each other.

Sunlight directly on eyes. Down to the floor boards. Dark wink in canopy bar shadow. Wink, wink, then the sun angled out of cockpit until the next turn, and the next, and the next.

Ben was hot. He was sweating. Hot from the exertion of maintaining the turn. Hot from the way his canopy acted like a greenhouse, trapping the sun's heat. Magnifying it. Hot from the heat of the *Merlin* engine inches in front of his feet. The engine had been at full power too long. The engine was hot. Ben guessed that the temperature gages were all in the high yellow, but he dared not look.

An unbidden, unpleasant thought came to Ben. What if he's better than I am? He's been perfect so far. Can I beat him? Is he a better pilot? Is the wrong mother's son going home today?

He forced himself away from the thought. To let the doubt remain would have been fatal. He settled to his task.

Details on the ground were becoming clearer. Farm fields, wood groves, houses and barns. They were getting low. He could make out individual trees, fences.

Was the German lower than he was? He looked like it. Only maybe 100 feet, but it would be enough. He snuck a glance at the ground. It was mostly flat. Only the stands of trees changed the ground elevation.

The two airplanes circled. Circled again.

Ben's arms ached. He was soaked. The mask hurt his nose. He was panting. He was fever hot. He did not notice any of it. All he saw was the black helmeted pilot, the black nosed *Messerschmitt* across the circle. He felt like he had spent hours staring at the top of the German's wings. He had come to hate the two black, geometric *Balkenkreuzes* painted on the splintered camouflage.

The ground was closer. Soon, one of them would have to break.

The German was lower. He broke.

When Ben saw the 109 roll out he knew he had won. He continued his hard turn for another half circle. When he rolled wings level he was behind the German – closing the distance between them. The German pilot tried to throw Ben off. His propeller was clipping corn stalks, flattening wheat. He pulled up to clear one stand of trees. Went around another. Ben stayed on his tail.

In his cockpit Ben had the gunsight pipper on the dodging *Messerschmitt*. Its wings touched the side of the range circle. Ben squeezed the trigger.

Only one machine gun fired.

He frantically looked down and checked switches. They were set correctly. All were on, yet only the far right side gun had fired.

They flew around more trees. Ben re-aimed. He fired again, the one gun sounding lonely as it sent out 600 bullets a minute. It only took a few seconds. 162 bullets. The *Messerschmitt* nosed over and smashed into the ground.

Ben kept *Suzy G* down low and headed west. The North Sea was an hour away. England an hour beyond that. He was exhausted. Over the relative safety of the North Sea, he unsnapped his mask and turned it over. A splash of spit, sweat and drool poured out. He wiped the mask on his thigh before putting it back on.

The big *Merlin* engine came to a stop as Ben pulled the red mixture knob back. *Suzy G*'s crew chief was on the wing pulling the canopy open. The armament sergeant stood in front of the right wing shaking his head at the tape over the muzzle opening on the inboard gun. He had already noticed the tape on both left guns. The outboard gun had soot streaked back on the top and bottom of the wing. The guns in the early model *Mustangs* had a problem. The laminar flow wing was too thin to install the Browning machine guns upright. They were leaned over to fit inside the wing. This meant the ammunition belts had to feed upward into the breeches. The ammo chutes were also somewhat too lightly built. While pulling G they jammed. After what Ben had put them through, it was a wonder any of the four fired at all. For the D model *Mustang*, the wing was thickened and six guns installed. They fit. The feed chutes were beefed up and the problem went away.

Even the warm summer air felt good as it came into the cockpit. Ben slumped against the seat back, braced his legs and lifted his ass off the seat for the first time in five and a half hours. "Geezus Lieutenant, whatta ya been doing," said the crew chief, "taking a swim? You're soaked."

Ben was wet. He tugged off his heavy leather flight gloves, black with sweat. His helmet was dark and wet. His socks inside his boots felt soggy. He was slow getting out of the cockpit.

"Hey Lieutenant, swing by the Doc's office and weigh yourself."

The Sergeant insisted and went with him. Peeled to his skivvies, he stood on the scale while a medic pushed the weight along the bar. Ben had lost nine pounds.

22

BOTTISHAM III

Promotion

On August 26 Ben Drew flew his personal airplane for the first time. In his log book, he wrote, "She's a beauty!"

Ben's *Mustang* was the latest model of P-51D with the fillet the pilots called a "B-17 tail" on the upper fin. Her USAAF serial number was 44-14164. The identification letters painted in black along the fuselage were E2*D. In the phonetics of the time, the airplane was "Easy two", as were all those of 375th squadron; "dog bar". D for Drew, but since a older P-51B was still flying as E2*D, the underline, or bar, was added to keep it distinctive.

Ben Drew with his Mustang, E2*D.
"Detroit Miss" is white with a black outline on a red bomb-shape.

Olive drab on the upper surfaces for camouflage, the group's distinctive yellow nose, now extended all the way back to the firewall, and the "Easy two dee bar" had already been painted on when the *Mustang* was delivered to his crew chief, Staff Sergeant Vernon Davis.

"Well, Lieutenant, what are you going to call her?" Sergeant Davis asked.

"I didn't really have anything in mind," said Ben, "Hadn't thought about it much."

"I know you're not married. You got a girlfriend?"

"No."

"How 'bout your mother?"

"It's an idea, but her name is Olive and she'd think it funny on an airplane."

"You ain't making this easy. Got a favorite song?"

"Heck, I like them all. I love to sing, " Ben said. "How about you? Do you have a girlfriend?"

"Nah. Besides, you're the one who flies her."

They both were silent for a few minutes.

"I know," the sergeant said finally, "What's your hometown?"

"I'm from Detroit."

"How 'bout we name her 'Detroit Miss'? I'll paint a big red bomb up here with 'Detroit Miss' lettered inside."

So was created one of the most famous individual aircraft of World War Two.

By the time he was given Detroit Miss, Ben had enough experience to know how he wanted his guns set. He had the inboard fifties aimed to converge at 200 yards, the middle guns at 250, and the outboards at 300 yards. A deadly concentration of fire over a long cone.

Bill Kemp knew what he was going to name his *Mustang*. His first P-51 was named "Betty Lee" after his wife. Unfortunately, the first "Betty Lee" did not last very long. After the mission where Kemp fought off the *Messerschmitts* to save the B-24 formation, she brought him home but was too damaged to continue. A new P-51D, serial 44-14270 became "Betty Lee II". Her name was painted in black script outlined with red on the yellow nose. The assistant crew chief's girlfriend's name, Marie, was in smaller letters well down on the side.

As a flight leader, Kemp was entitled to have his initial as the last letter in his airplane's identification. However, E2*K was already being used by the group commander, Colonel Joe Kruzel in his *Mustang* "Vi". "Vi" had unique markings because of Kruzel's record. There were both Japanese and Nazi flags as victory markings on her canopy frame. E2*X was available, would Kemp like that? X resembles K, but it was the finality, the symbol of a score that decided Kemp. "Betty Lee II" was "Easy Two Xray".

Bill Kemp's second Mustang, E2*X.

As combat pilots in the thick of the action, the *Katzenjammer Kids* garnered their share of medals and formal awards. Ben's first Air Medal was awarded on August 6, 1944. An Oak Leaf Cluster followed on August 15. There was no ceremony. He went by the squadron office and picked the box off a pile. What was memorable was his next award.

September 5th meant nothing special. A typical non-mission day at Bottisham. Ben felt the call of nature, swiped a *Yank* magazine that was laying around, and headed for the latrine. He was comfortably enthroned and thumbing through *Yank* when he heard someone come in. There were metal, GI, urinals on the first section of wall with stainless steel sinks opposite. The other section had a row of five plywood stalls for the commodes. To improve ventilation the walls of the stalls did not reach all the way to the ceiling. The stall doors were shorter still with the bottom edge eighteen inches off the wooden floor. All wood surfaces except the floor were painted a bilious green.

"Hey. Is Lieutenant Drew in here?"

Ben recognized the voice of Sergeant Cruikshank, the intelligence assistant from mission debriefings.

"Yeah, Sarge. I'm down here." What in the world do they want with me now?, was his thought. Can't a guy even use the bathroom in peace?

"Down where?"

"Down here. Uh, third stall."

"OK. Got something for you."

Ben could see Cruikshank's shoes under the door.

"Here. Catch."

A small box covered with blue leatherette sailed over the top. Ben dropped the magazine on his legs and caught it with two hands. The inside of the slim box was lined with blue satin. A blue flocked piece of cardboard was bent and cut to hold the medal and its ribbon. The ribbon was red, white and blue stripes. The medal was bronze with a prominent four bladed propeller. The Distinguished Flying Cross. The DFC was the dream of every American combat pilot.

Sergeant Cruikshank was on his way out. "Phee-yeew! This place stinks. Oh... congratulations Lieutenant."

Not only were there medals, but at the beginning of September, despite the disciplinary action hanging over their heads, Urban L. Drew and William T. Kemp were promoted to the rank of First Lieutenant in the United States Army Air Forces. Their base pay jumped to one hundred and sixty-six dollars a month. Add 50% for flight pay and 10% for overseas allowance and they were relatively rich in the days of nickel beer.

The nature of the bombing campaign had shifted. The Eighth Air Force routinely sent hundreds of heavy bombers on deep penetration missions into Germany, Czechoslovakia, Poland, Austria. Short range missions into France became rare as Allied troops pushed the Germans out. For the fighter pilots, this meant long missions in single seat airplanes. The groans heard when the intelligence officers pulled back the curtain on the briefing board and the length of tape marking the route to the target appeared were not of fear of the enemy, but anticipation of what their backsides would feel like before the mission was over. Drew, Kemp and the other hard-chargers in the 361st liked the long missions despite the personal discomfort – the more time over the enemy's home land, the more chances to fight.

Long missions meant early briefings and early briefings meant even earlier wake-ups. The intelligence staff who had the task of waking the pilots soon learned that Billy Kemp was hazardous to be near. A newly arrived, newly commissioned lieutenant was clipped hard by a Kemp haymaker and from that morning on, carried a broom handle to nudge the ex-boxer awake from a safe distance.

There were unexpected hazards from your own side in the air as well.

Ben was leading his flight of four *Mustangs* and about to join up with the bomber formation they were assigned to when an unknown voice called, "Break!"

Without hesitation, he popped the stick right and stomped rudder. His wingman matched his move. Number three and four broke left. The two sections scissored across in a maneuver designed to clear each others' tails. Anxious eyes scanned the sky high, low, left, right. There were no enemy fighters. The sky was clear except for the bombers.

Ben reversed his turn, reduced his bank angle. Three and four closed back into escort formation.

"All right," Ben said on the radio, "who called 'break'?"

Silence.

He keyed the mike again. "Listen, whoever called 'break', if you saw bogies, fine, but next time call their location."

A quiet voice came back, "Sorry, White Leader, but I saw tracers coming by."

Ben knew where the tracers were from. He had seen this problem before. As he closed with the bombers a second time – slowly, showing lots of profile, as he was always careful to do – he switched to the radio frequency common to bombers and fighters. "Lissen up, Bomb Leader, if you can't keep better control of your gunners, you can damn well go to Germany all by yourselves."

If it were possible for machinery to look embarrassed, several round ball and half-dome top turrets did as they swung their pairs of guns away from their "little friends."

To Ben, becoming a flight leader was something he felt he deserved. He could fly and fight. He had shot down Germans. Soon after becoming the leader of A Flight, he learned there were other aspects to his position.

A new replacement was assigned to A Flight. The youngster had done well on local familiarization flights and mock combats. The need for pilots was such that he did not spend time as a "floater". He was assigned to A Flight for his first combat missions. The first one, he complained of a rough running engine and turned back over the Channel. The mechanics found nothing wrong with the *Merlin*. The next mission he was to go on was a long, rough one – deep into Germany. He again turned back with a rough runner. Again, the mechs found nothing wrong.

One, even two, turn-backs could happen. By the third, it was time for his flight leader to talk to him. Ben was his flight leader.

The kid was alone in the Nissen Hut. Empty bunks with green blankets reached to the ends of the hut. Ben had creases across his face from goggles and oxygen mask. He had come straight from debriefing. He even skipped the gun-camera film showing.

The kid had his head in his hands. He was crying. Ben did not know what to do. He sat on the next bunk, hands on knees, helmet dangling from one hand. "Well, do you want to talk about it?"

"Oh, sir. Sir, you don't know what I'm going through." Sir? Ben Drew was twenty years old. The new man, the same. "Here, look." The young man stood and wiped his face with the back of his hand. He opened his locker and removed a pack of letters. He sat down and unfolded one of the flimsy, air mail pages, handed it to Ben.

Ben read the page. He read another letter. By the third, he understood. Passages sprang out at him; "Killing is evil…, you will burn in hell if you shoot anyone…, Remember the commandants, …you are not my son, if you kill."

Mrs. Olive Drew signed all her letters to her son, "Good Hunting."

Ben had always assumed all pilots were like him. Eager to fight. Victory counted, death only a consequence. Your family was behind you… all the way.

The kid was not a simple case of fear or nerves. How did one deal with a situation like his?

Ben talked to people he could trust. Not simply the chain-of-command – the air force bureaucracy would have chopped the youngster up. He talked to men who cared, men who understood. The resolution was a happy one. Rather than having his wings pulled, the troubled pilot was transferred to the Air Transport Command. There he could use his pilot skills without his mother's condemnation.

23

LITTLE WALDEN

September Song

Airfields on the continent were coming under allied control. A *Marauder* medium bomber group was moved to France to be closer to their interdiction targets. The move left Little Walden empty. The 361 Fighter Group transferred there. In a remarkably smooth transition, the fighters took-off from Bottisham on an escort mission and landed at Little Walden. Their new home had the advantage of smooth, concrete runways. The pilots were glad to be rid of the slippery PSP.

September 11 and 12 were good days for the *Katzenjammer Kids*. They were flight leaders and had their new P-51D's with *Detroit Miss* and *Betty Lee II* emblazoned on the yellow noses. They were ready to live up to the reputation the PR flacks had created for the *Katzenjammers* and, at the same time, continue their private contest. Two days in a row they each found more Germans for their guns. Indeed, it would prove to be an adventurous couple of days for all the 375th.

On 11 September, the 375th escorted *Liberators* of the 448th Bomb Group of the 20th Combat Wing to Magdeburg in the center of Germany. The B-24s twin vertical tails were painted a bright insignia yellow with a broad black band running down from the front corner. A white letter "T" was in the center. On the right wing, as if to balance the national star and bar insignia on the left, was a black circle with a white dash.

The bomb run had gone well and the factory area was nothing but billowing clouds of black and brown as the three mile long formation of "Heavies" turned ponderously west for home.

The 375th was allowed to sweep ahead. Other squadrons would cover the bombers' withdrawal.

South of Gottingen, Ben spotted an Me 109 doing aerobatics over, into and under a large cumulo-nimbus cloud. The dark green fighter was in sharp contrast to the glaring white. Second Lieutenant Seymour Beder was Ben's wingman. As scheduled this time, unlike the Rostock mission. They had to squint against the dazzle to keep their quarry in sight.

Ben thought, *what the hell is this guy doing? There's Yank fighters all over the place. Where's his wingman?*

Ben banked *Detroit Miss* and craned his head around to check behind. He looked over at his wingman. Beder was doing all right for a new guy. He was to Ben's side, banking the opposite way to weave under. His head was moving. If there were airplanes behind them, he would see them. Ben resumed the chase, diving at an angle to close the range.

The German pilot saw the *Mustangs* closing and headed for the nearest bulge of cloud. He would use it to hide and get away.

Ben knew just what to do. He gave a quick hand wave and said, "White two, stay clear," on the radio. He did a fast turn to a heading he guessed would take him out of the cloud at the same place as the German, leveled his wings and got on the gages. Just in time. He was concentrating on the attitude gyro and compass when he hit the cumulous with a bump and all outside references vanished. Cumulous clouds are puffy because of energetic air currents. It was a rough ride. Ben knew he was diving, but had plenty of altitude. He held his heading. As speed built up he needed left rudder to keep the ball centered. He pushed automatically. In a moment, it became lighter and he popped out of the cloud. In the bright of blue and white, his eyes took a long instant to find the *Messerschmitt*.

There he is. He's doing acrobatics again! Either he's a very senior and expert ace, having himself a ball playing with me. Or he's nuts.

The *Luftwaffe* pilot finished a roll to the right and pulled up into a wingover reversal. At the top, he must have seen the *Mustang* below and behind him for he kept his nose down and dived back into the cloud. Ben followed him.

Again the bumps and wet greyness. This time, when the two airplanes hit clear air, they were much closer. Ben above instead of below. Since he was at the far limits of fifty caliber machine guns, Ben put the pipper high on his target. The German rolled again and was belly up when the six streams of bullets tore into him. They punched through the aluminum skin and up into the cockpit. It was a long burst. Chunks of metal flew off the 109. Without a hand pushing the stick to one side, the roll slowed noticeably. The propeller slowed as the nose came up. The airplane shuddered and fell off into a spin.

The chase and dives through the clouds had taken the fighters down to a lower altitude. The *Messerschmitt* started its spin at eleven hundred feet. It did not take long to hit the ground. It exploded when it hit and burned with heavy black smoke.

Ben swung around and came back over the wreckage with his trigger at the first click so the gun camera would work without firing the guns. Off to the side, he saw that his wingman was coming back into formation. The wreckage was still burning when they climbed up to the bomber formation. *Detroit Miss* had her first victory. It was Ben Drew's fourth.

On another mission that September, a damaged *Liberator* had slipped behind. Ben led his flight over to escort it to safety. In order to keep their speed up, yet stay with the slow bomber, they a were weaving overhead – a standard practice. Crossing into Holland, Ben watched as John Lougheed banked to turn back across the lone B-24. The *Mustang* was not as high as it should have been for separation. As he watched, the bank angle steepened. The *Mustang* was going to smash into the bomber. Almost inverted, it hit the huge fin and rudder on the right, twisted down on the elevator and rear turret. The fighter came away from the bomber a spinning mass of flaming wreckage. The *Liberator* slewed to the left and nosed over. Ben watched for chutes. He saw nine parachutes open. Somehow the B-24 stayed upright and bellied-in near Ommen in Holland.

There was never an explanation of what had happened. The best guess was Lougheed's oxygen mask had come loose or had malfunctioned. He became hypoxic and lost control. The *Liberator*'s tail gunner was killed, but mercifully, the remaining nine members of the crew survived. It was one of those senseless reminders that even without the enemy, flying war planes was hazardous.

The long – for a fighter in combat – career of the *Suzy G* came to an end that day. One of the first *Mustang*s to be delivered to the 375th Fighter Squadron, she had flown over the Normandy beaches on D-Day. She looked pretty as the only B model P-51 in the famous color photo taken in July. Her "birdcage" canopy had been replaced with a clear bubble "Malcolm" hood. Two weeks before, Ben Drew had flown *Suzy G* in his fierce, one on one dogfight near Rostok. This day, she wound up in a field of cabbages at Thorpe Park, near Clacton in Essex. Her back broken, she would never fly again. Ironically, her pilot, First Lieutenant. Francis Glankler, was back in the states on leave between tours during her last flight. A new replacement pilot had brought her back to England. He walked away from the crash.

The day after, the 375th went to Magedeburg again. This time as escorts for the Third Bomb Division's B-17s. Ben remained at Bottisham while *Detroit Miss* was being repaired. In between wandering the ops room and standing on the tower for the group's return, he flew a one hour check flight on Easy Two Dee Bar. He hated missing even one chance to go after the *Luftwaffe*. Kemp's success made staying behind worse.

Success at air combat is the experience, training and talent to do everything exactly right and fast. Bill Kemp did just that on 12 September, 1944.

The *Flying Fortresses* of the Third Division were the most colorful in the 8th. The all yellow tails and black squares indicated it was the 4th Wing flying below. Kemp was leading D flight at 25,000 feet ten miles from Magdeburg when he spotted a formation of a dozen *Messerschmitt 109s* crossing under their formation. There were moments of hesitation as squadron and *staffel* leaders evaluated position and altitude. The space below the crossing formations was sprinkled with drop tanks as pilots jettisoned their own when their leaders' came off. One from each German, two from each American fighter.

Kemp was first in. He chose one of the attackers and fired. A short burst from 200 yards out. Pieces came from the wing roots, a glittery cloud from the canopy. The canopy flew off. The *Luftwaffe* pilot jumped seconds later. Kemp looked up and pulled. Fired a longer burst. From in close, dead astern, 200 yards. His bullets tore into a second enemy fighter, sparkling as they pierced the aluminum. The 109 snapped into a spin. It kept spinning all the way into the ground. Kemp rolled left and looked around. He reversed his controls and looked right. Down low, there was a *Mustang* with a *Messerschmitt* on his tail. Kemp's stick went forward, his throttle though the "gate". The dive was steep. Airspeed high. His controls stiffened, but he was getting closer. He fired a burst. The tracers warned the German who kept diving for the trees. As the *Messerschmitt* leveled off it slowed. Kemp got closer. He fired short, quick bursts at his jinking target. He hit him. Hit him again. The *Messerschmitt* headed down from fifty feet. Both wings tore off in the trees. The rest exploded on the ground.

First Lieutenant. Kemp had gone from 25,000 feet to the deck, shot down three Me 109s, all in less than seven minutes. They were his first victories in *Betty Lee II*.

In addition, the 375th squadron commanding officer, Major Charles Cummins, in his *Mustang* named *Geraldine*, and Lieutenants Narvis and Knupp had each destroyed an enemy fighter. It had been a good couple of days for the squadron. And for the *Katzenjammer Kids*.

The score was Drew-four, Kemp-six.

Bill Kemp after scoring a triple.

24

BALTIC SEA

Monster Boat

What a remarkable day that was for me.

We were escorting B-17s on a shuttle mission to Russia. The missions were code named "Frantic" and were quite an operation. I later learned three were flown altogether. The last, September 11, was the only one I was on. They were all major efforts. All seventy-five Fortresses *of the 1st Bomb Division, made up the attack force. Instead of bombing and returning to England, they would drop their loads and continue on into the Soviet Union. This way they could attack targets in Eastern Germany and Poland. A couple of days later, the Russians would load them and they'd reverse the process. An entire American fighter wing would provide the escort. On this mission, the target was Chemnitz. The fighters, all Mustangs, were lead by Colonel Don Blakeslee, commander of the 4th Fighter Group. The practice was to send one group all the way to Russia with the bombers, while somewhere off the south coast of Sweden, Soviet fighters would rendezvous and take up the balance of the escort. The rest of us – some six fighter groups – would return home, to England.*

We had turned west. There had been no enemy activity so far, and with that number of fighters along, the prospect of any action was remote. I was doing my usual search of the ground as well as the sky, looking for targets when I thought I saw something.

It was another of those missions when A flight was only three of us. I don't remember what happened to the fourth man, but Travis and Rogers were on my wing. I asked for permission to peel off and investigate a bogey. Cheerful leader said to go ahead.

I turned north and started a long dive. Sweden had remained neutral throughout the war. A fair number of shot-up airplanes wound up there and both the allies and Germans ran courier flights in and out. At least that's what I assume the Heinkel was. There was little other reason for it to be that far out over the Baltic.

The Heinkel 111 was flying low, hugging the wave tops, hoping to stay out of sight. But I'd spotted him. The bomber was camouflaged in standard Luftwaffe light and very dark green. No special markings were visible. If he'd spotted my flight, he gave no indication; he kept flying straight for the Reich.

I had built up pretty good speed in the dive and with the sky clear, I set up for a textbook tail attack. Felt like I was back at Bartow. With one important difference; here I could drop directly behind him and shoot which was, of course, absolutely forbidden on a towed target. The He-111 didn't have a tail turret – none of the German airplanes did. Two of the gunners could shoot to the rear, but the one in the belly bathtub could only shoot low, and since the One-eleven was less than a hundred feet, I certainly wasn't going below it. And the upper gunner's field of fire was blocked by his own tail. Directly at six o'clock was a good place to attack a lone He111.

It was too easy. An absolutely no deflection shot. My first burst set his right engine on fire. Suddenly, my whole windscreen was full of Heinkel. I yanked back on the stick to avoid a collision. Gave the top gunner a chance to spray me, but he missed. I felt like an idiot. I had forgotten just how slow the Heinkel was. The 111 first flew in 1935… and it showed.

I banked hard right and reversed to kill my speed and come back in. Over the radio, I heard, "We've got him, White Lead.*"*

"The hell you do," I shouted back, "this bastard's mine."

I could see muzzle flashes from the top machine gun as I came back down. I put the pipper on the big cockpit greenhouse and held the trigger down. I had shifted my aim to the left engine when the Heinkel *nosed over and hit the water with a big splash. I led the guys in a circle over the spot, but there was nothing left except a few pieces of debris and disturbed water.*

The coast wasn't far away, so I only climbed a couple of thousand feet to look for targets to strafe. I could barely believe what I found.

Not too far past the Polish coast, there's a large lake, Lake Schall. The Germans had a seaplane base there that I knew about. Figured to shoot up some float planes or amphibs. As we got closer to the lake, I saw this giant flying boat sitting there. It wasn't moving. Just tied to a buoy. Couple of small boats on the water nearby. It was in standard green camouflage with obvious black and white crosses on wings and fuselage. It was the biggest airplane I had ever seen. The monster had six engines.

Travis and Rogers had spread out behind me so we all came in at different angles. Talk about a target you couldn't miss. And we didn't. I saw my bullets hitting wings and center fuselage as I flew over. Travis, as number two, and Rogers, the last one over, shot off almost all they had. I didn't risk a second run. The Flak *gunners at the airbase had opened up with everything they had and there were tracers and explosions all around us. Besides, as I pulled up and away, I looked back and saw Rogers finish his run. By then, the monster flying boat was a mass of flame and noticeably lower in the water. We climbed high and headed back to Little Walden*

Mission debrief was a riot. All the three of us could talk about was the giant flying boat. It was some time before we got around to my Heinkel *kill.*

Houston pulled out the recognition manuals and we flipped through pages looking for an airplane that looked like the one we shot up. The closest thing to what we remembered was the Blohm and Voss 222, Viking. *Not exact, but close. It was a six engined flying boat. 120 feet long, 150 foot wingspan. A huge airplane. I, we, were thrilled to have burned and sunk one.*

Eighth Air Force rules allowed only two "destroyed" claims for each target, so I gave Travis and Rogers the Destroyed credit and took a Damage claim on what we assumed to be a BV222. After all, I had the confirmed He111.

Need I say, we were impatient to see the gun camera films.

Each of our films was pretty good. You would think with three sets, a positive ident would have been possible. Vibration from the six firing guns was usually a problem as it made it difficult to see detail. The best stuff came when the pilot had the chance – and remembered – to press down only a bit on the trigger to activate the camera without firing. Almost none of us ever did.

But these films were good. We could see it had six engines and was generally shaped like the Viking flying boat. But there was this feeling that something didn't quite match the profiles and photos, the drawings of the 222.

We ran the film several times, including trying to analyze the really fuzzy images in stop frame, but learned nothing more before heading to the club to celebrate our victories.

The score was Drew-five, Kemp-six.

The Blohm and Voss BV-238

25

FRANCE

Mistake?

Ben Drew shot an American airplane to smithereens. Or thought he had. Or, more accurately, thought he was responsible for his wingman shooting an American airplane to smithereens.

I never forgot the Spitfire incident. It was not the sort of thing you could forget. Bad enough that I almost was killed by an RAF fighter in revenge for our blowing one of theirs out of the sky. It was a horrible mistake. I learned for myself just how hard it must have been for Johnson. I found out how terrible shooting one of your own could be.

As A Flight commander, I was on a Ramrod at a time when the front lines were very mobile. General George Patton was on his way to becoming a legend. His Third Army was moving fast, rolling the Germans back to the "fatherland." We were always briefed on the best guess as to where the lines were before each mission. But with Patton, we'd go out one day and be in the right area. By the next day Patton had moved his columns fifty miles, or more. You'd think you had crossed the lines, but with Patton's rolling Third, you could never be sure.

My wingman was Lee Travis who had been on the mission over the Baltic Sea a few days before.

Ben had asked for, and received permission to take "A" flight down on the deck to strafe targets of opportunity. The *Mustang*s, call sign "Yellow Flight", crossed a large open field, one hundred feet over the green grass. Ben scanned the tree line at the far side. He spotted a twin engine airplane. "Yellow Two, there's an airplane parked under those trees. Pull out to the right and we'll come around again and shoot the bastard."

Ben was certain he'd led his flight well across the battle-line. He was certain he had seen what had to be a *Junkers 88* or *Heinkel 111* in the shadows.

He followed Travis around in a sweeping turn to the right. Because of the arc of the turn, he had lagged behind and was slightly off track to the twin-engined airplane he had spotted. His wingman was dead on.

The *Mustang's* wings lit up as the fifties fired. Five men were standing in front of the airplane under the trees. Five men went down as bullets tore into them. Travis lifted his aim and the slugs ate into the airplane shadowed beneath the trees. It started to burn.

I was heading in at an angle to get a crack at it myself. About the time he opened up, I got a good look. Saw it was a C-47. A Dakota. A Gooney Bird. American, or at least Brit. And Travis took out the guys standing in front of it. I yelled, "Hold your fire. Hold your fire! It's ours. It's one of ours." But by that time he'd put a couple hundred rounds into a Douglas, made-in-the USA, C-47.

He and I pulled up. He slid back into wing position. Three and four joined up and we headed for home. The radios were awfully quiet all the way back.

The pilots went to the brick ops building at Little Walden for debriefing. Captain Larry Houston was the Squadron Intelligence Officer. It was his job to write down the details as each pilot remembered them and try to compose a complete, and accurate, picture of what really happened in the hectic moments of aerial combat. He sent his reports to higher commands where other intelligence officers put his reports together with reports from all the squadrons, then all the fighter wings, and the bomber commands of the Eighth Air Force to try to see what really happened. Those reports went higher still, to the joint allied commands, where reports from the RAF, Air Sea Rescue, the American and British Armies on the ground in France, and a myriad of allied units were merged into what really happened.

Intelligence Officers were both despised and admired. They were the men who days later came back and said that the sure kill had not gone down, or was a shared claim, or could not be located. They were also the men who credited kills "officially". The men who wrote the citations for the medals, the honors.

Larry Houston had been a lawyer in New York City before the war. Despite his being a ground-pounder and their initial run-in at Bottisham, he was one of Ben's closest pals. A large part of it was Larry's open disgust with higher Headquarters. He frequently, and too loudly, would say, "All that group wants to do is get promoted. All they want to do is be career officers after the war; all they're doing is pushing rank. Worthless bastards."

Ben stood, near the folding table that Houston used as a desk, uncharacteristically quiet, while the other flight leaders gave their versions of what they each thought really happened. The others left the tent to wait for gun camera films, talk to their crew chiefs, shower, catch a nap, get an early beer.

Larry Houston laid his pen down, straightened the pile of debriefing forms, and neatly placed a new, blank one on top. 'What's the matter Drew? You don't look as happy as you usually do."

"Captain, I think I'm in deep trouble."

The other members of "A" flight were ranged around the tent – as quiet as Ben had been. Lee Travis, his wingman, the one who had shot up the airplane, was studying the toes of his boots as though they were crown jewels. And all the jewels in the world would not make him look up.

"OK. Start from the beginning. What happened?"

Ben didn't start from the beginning. Usually, he was the best debriefer of all the pilots; he remembered details, he knew where he was, at what time. That afternoon, he was close to incoherent. He talked a rambling monologue. Larry Houston let him. He was smart. He would work out what really happened.

"Jesus, Captain. All the way home, I can't get the thought out of my skull, Drew boy, you are really in the deep stuff now. Damn. I mean deeep shit. We killed those guys standing by that airplane. Shot the shit out of 'em. It was a C-47. No doubt about it. Captain, you know, I know, my aircraft identification is pretty damned good. It was a C-47. A built in the USA, C-47. Douglas Aircraft. California. Not a *Junkers*. Not a *Heinkel*. A C-47. I saw him under the trees. Called it. We came back around, shot the shit out of it. Five guys. Shot 'em up. Too late, saw it was a C-47. What was a 47 doing there? Christ, we were way over the lines. I'm sure of it. Too late. Called it too late. Too late..."

Ben stopped, worn out. Houston was older than the pilots. He'd been around. He also hadn't been there holding a trigger down.

Slowly, firmly, he said, "Let's keep it in the squadron for the moment. I'll contact SHAEF headquarters... quietly. And Eighth Air Force headquarters too. Find out who lost a C-47 today. Check with the Ninth Air Force too. Maybe one of theirs, was in the area. Whole thing doesn't make sense. I agree, you were far past our lines. Even Patton isn't that far."

It took a month. No C-47s were missing. None. No Americans, no British. It took time to check all the possibilities. No one at any headquarters, at any staff could find any lost airplanes. The 8th Air Force headquarters really went into it when they heard it was a C-47, but they found nothing. So, officially, they said it had to have been a captured airplane. Captured by the Germans months before. Maybe in

Italy. So Ben was right to shoot it up. The guys killed were Germans – had to be. There were no Americans lost, no allied transports lost that day. What really happened was never known, but Ben was relieved. Although he had not fired at the airplane, he had ordered the attack. It made no difference he was a mere lieutenant. He was the flight leader. The leader. He was responsible.

26

HAMM

First Encounter

The marker flares were spinning their corkscrew smoke trails down over Hamm, Germany. The pilot of the lead bomber had leveled his wings and started on his bomb run with thirty-six more heavies right behind him when Ben spotted an unknown aircraft cross 10,000 feet below his flight. The three *Mustangs* of "A" flight were at 20,000 with the rest of the 375th covering the bombers during their run over the target.

Ben Drew called *Cadet Leader* and was given permission to go down on a bounce. All Ben could tell was that the bogie was a twin engined airplane flying 90 degrees to his heading. There was fuel remaining in his drop tanks so he left them on until he knew the situation. Behind him, strings of 500 pound general purpose bombs tumbled from the B-24s.

Ben was not flying *Detroit Miss* this day. He was in E2*I, which was also a new P-51D. His swooping descent pointed him in front of the *bogie* and in a 60 degree dive. The throttle was at full power and the airspeed building up. He had not gained a foot on the two engined airplane.

Ben pickled off his drop tanks.

The *Mustang* accelerated to 500 miles per hour and still did not get any closer to the diving *bogie*. Ben noticed occasional puffs of smoke which confirmed his suspicion that the *bogie* was one of the new jet propelled aircraft the pilots had been hearing about.

"Cadet Leader, this Blue Leader. I'm chasing one of those jet jobs," Ben said, "and I'm not having much luck catching him."

The *Mustang*s and the jet had maintained their dives and were less than a thousand feet from the ground. Ben shoved his throttle into full combat power to get more speed. It made no apparent difference. Ben decided to give up and eased the throttle back.

The dark painted jet went into a shallow turn to the right.

Ben shoved the throttle back up. Whipped into a hard right bank and cut inside the jet's turn. The range was closing nicely when the jet's pilot must have seen the yellow nosed *Mustang*, because he steepened his turn. At their closest point, the airplanes were ninety degrees to each other. It was an impossible shot, but Ben squeezed the trigger anyway.

Normally in a steep, hard turn an airplane bleeds off airspeed. This did not seem to be the case – the jet was as fast as before.

Ben was at least close enough that he could identify it as a *Messerschmitt 262*. Until now, all he had seen was drawings of what the new jet was supposed to look like. With this encounter he became one of the first half dozen American pilots to fly against the *Me 262*. And so far, he was both impressed and frustrated by its speed. So were both his wingmen.

The *Messerschmitt* sped along low with the three *Mustang*s trailing behind. Every time the jet banked, Ben fired using what slight lead he could get. He tried aiming high to give his bullets time to reach the target, but pulling his nose up, even a few degrees, cost him airspeed. He kept shooting – partly out of frustration, partly hoping for a lucky shot.

Another *Messerschmitt 262* appeared high and to the right, but swooped off in a wide arc. His wingman turned after it.

The *Luftwaffe* pilot headed for an aerodrome. When Ben saw the enemy airfield, he called his flight and told them to hug the deck. The German was trying to drag the Americans into a *Flak* trap. They were at 1500 feet and going 450 miles an hour. Although he started a sharp right turn, the *Flak* remained heavy... and accurate.

Ben saw one of his wingman hit and bailout. He lost contact with the other one. Directly on his nose was a small railroad marshaling yard with its thick clusters of anti-aircraft guns. He was going too fast to miss it. The *Flak* came from all directions.

The jet was still ahead of him and flying on a fairly straight course. When it started another shallow turn, Ben thought he had another chance and started firing from a 1,000 yards, but he was out of range and did not get any hits. Looking around, Ben reviewed his situation; the jet was trying to lead him back to the airfield with its *Flak* batteries, there were many *Luftwaffe* single-engine fighters airborne and heading for him, he had fired all his ammunition except a couple hundred rounds, and his wingmen were missing. Enough was enough. He headed west, climbed, figured out where he was and headed for home base.

MESSERSCHMITT 262
The pure fighter version was called *Schwalbe*, Swallow. The fighter bomber, which had bomb racks on the fuselage was called *Stürmvögel*, Stormy Petrel. (Late in the war, Me262's were delivered unpainted with the sealant for the seams obvious…and sloppy looking.)

The wingman who had turned after the second Me262 was Second Lieutenant Bob McCandliss and he was more frustrated than his flight leader. At least Drew had been shooting.

Robert K. McCandliss had attended MIT for two years before enlisting in the Air Corps. After waiting for a callup date and being delayed by a serious case of viral pneumonia, he finally made it to England in August of '44 and was assigned to the 375th fighter squadron. His first missions had been with a variety of leaders. He was a "floater" longer than most. Even without being assigned a flight, he was given a P-51B with a cage canopy – E2*M. He did not have her long enough to name her. Within three days, a new guy lost oil pressure and had to bailout of E2*M on a practice flight.

He quickly learned who the aggressive flight leaders were and who were the ones who somehow seemed to avoid engaging the enemy. The *Katzenjammer Kids* were the favorite flight leaders for any pilot who wanted action. Billy Kemp lived in the same hut as he did. One evening, Kemp came back from the Officers' Club and fired four shots into the ceiling with his 45 automatic. Uncivilized behavior anywhere but in a fighter squadron. McCandliss was hooked up with the other *Katzenjammer*. He was overjoyed to be was assigned as Ben Drew's full time wingman because Ben was known for "going in harm's way."

McCandliss's background and training were in engineering. He loved machinery and was a natural tinkerer. Soon after his arrival in the 375th, he realized the airplanes he was assigned usually had a history of mechanical problems. The squadron Engineering Officer, who was in charge of the mechanics and maintaining the airplanes, was a graduate of Purdue's engineering program. Captain Cowell also lived in the same Nissen hut; the third bunk down from McCandliss. Their engineering backgrounds gave them a lot in common and they would get into discussions that were technical enough to have the other pilots looking for a drink or magazine. When McCandliss chided him about the quality of the airplanes he flew, Cowell grinned and said, "You're the only one I can trust to read the gauges right. I know that if I give you an airplane with a problem, you're the best pilot around to figure out not only what's wrong, but be able to write it up so it makes sense."

So McCandliss flew a lot of *Mustangs* which had been repaired or recently modified. This may also have been the reason he frequently had the latest gadgets in his airplane.

At Hamm he was in a P-51B. This model *Mustang* had been in use since the 361st group had converted from Thunderbolts in May, but they were kept in fighting shape. Most had received the bubble like Malcolm hood in place of the original birdcage canopy to improve visibility. Some had the newly developed Mark-14 gyro tracking gunsight which had begun arriving in Europe and Captain Cowell had one installed in the airplane McCandliss was flying.

Instead of the fixed circle and dot, the gyro sight had a ring of diamonds that were adjustable to assist in determining range and moved with the aiming pipper. Both were driven by an internal gyroscope which sensed lateral displacement rates and computed lead angle automatically.

When he spotted the second *Messerschmitt* at four o'clock, McCandliss had banked around hard to go after him. Over the radio he called for permission to go after the second bogey. He got no reply.

McCandliss uncaged the gyro sight, put the pipper and diamonds on the speeding jet and watched the fixed reticle waver and twitch far in front of the Me 262. The gunsight was computing lead for the huge angle of deflection. Now, all he had to do was get in range of his guns. McCandliss called again for clearance to continue the chase. "I've got a shot, *Blue Leader*. Long range, but I have a shot." Again, there was no reply. As he described the chase later, "It was like trying to catch a motorcycle while on a bicycle."

The jet was pulling away so McCandliss turned back into the formation as a good wingman should. His dodge to the side had put him into the number three position.

He watched the smoke trails from *Blue Leader's* guns as Ben futilely shot again at the first *Messerschmitt*. As the flight came closer to the airfield, he radioed the airplane in front of him to watch the *Flak*. There was no acknowledgment.

He watched white smoke coming from the wings of Lieutenant Danny Knupp's *Mustang*. At first he thought that Knupp was shooting at something, but the bursts were too irregular. Knupp was being shot at... and hit. Knupp was flying the number two position. His position.

In seconds, Knupp's *Mustang* rolled inverted and dove toward the ground at a 45 degree angle. Somehow, Knupp managed to bail out before the airplane crashed and exploded.

McCandliss circled wide and watched Knupp land near the intersection of two roads. He was OK. McCandliss made two passes over the intersection to distract any Germans close by and give Knupp time to hide. However, over his radio he heard other members of the squadron calling out 109s and 190s around him. There were a lot.

To get away, McCandliss headed for a fat, puffy cumulus cloud nearby. Before entering the glaring white, he held wings level and uncaged his attitude gyro. Flying completely on instruments, he spiraled up, hidden by cloud.

At 15,000 feet, he popped out and saw a bomber stream nearby escorted by a flight of P-51s which still had their drop tanks attached. He started toward them, but found an unidentified *Mustang*, like him, without tanks, and joined up for the flight back.

The usual procedure was to cross the Channel fairly high in case something went wrong, but the stranger he was with did a buzz job all the way across. McCandliss stayed at 500 feet and kept him in sight until approaching the English coast. Then he climbed and came up on the radio asking for a homing steer. The heading he heard sounded strange, but he took it.

The first landmark he recognized was the city of London. A long way from Bottisham. He had less than fifteen gallons of gas. Wanting to have some fuel for landing, he looked for the nearest airfield. He was in luck; he was lined up with a runway.

Any port in a storm. McCandliss did not care at that point where he was. He simply wanted to be on the ground. Running out of gas in the air is definitely not like running out in a car – you can't coast over to the side of the road. He landed and taxied toward the blocky operations building and control tower. He passed a row of C-47s. *Gooney Birds*. Transports. He opened his canopy, nonchalantly rested his arm on the rail. Held his head up higher.

Past the *Gooney Birds* was a cluster of CG-4s, parked pointing every which way. Bulbous, ugly, cellophane and fabric gliders. Gliders! No engines at all. Flown by semi-washouts. Guys who couldn't hack it in fighters, or even, bombers. He was at a transport base. An ATC base. ATC was actually Air Transport Command, but McCandliss remembered all the jokes, beginning when he was selected for fighter training: ATC meant Allergic To Combat, Army of Terrified Copilots. No copilots for him. No gliders which sank like lead. It had taken an unauthorized dogfight at an illegal altitude over a church in a trainer, to show the powers-that-be he had the right spirit. The misdeed cost him hours of sweat, wondering if his entire flying career was over, but had been worth it. He was a Fighter Pilot. He zipped his leather jacket open, pulled out his white silk scarf and let the fringed end blow in the slipstream.

A crowd had gathered by the ops building to see why a P-51 had landed at their base. McCandliss came in fast, pressed hard on the left brake, jazzed the *Merlin*, and spun smartly into a parking spot.

Naturally, he did not want to turn his back to his audience, to climb awkwardly out of the cockpit, so he braced his hands on windscreen and canopy and jumped straight onto the wing. He slipped. Both feet went out from under. He crashed on his back. Lay there flat on his ass while the transport and glider pilots laughed.

All the high power operation and maneuvering had caused the *Merlin* to blow oil all over the nose and inner wing. It was a much subdued Lieutenant McCandliss who returned to Bottisham. The ATC had been only too happy to give the "hotshot" fighter pilot gas and oil.

At Bottisham, the mechs checked out his radio. The transmitter was not working. It probably had not the entire flight. He had an explanation for why Drew never answered him, for why he got an erroneous steer. It was not what McCandliss needed to hear after his embarrassment at the ATC base.

27

ACHMER

Shooting Swallows

I always believed in low flying. Call it buzzing, flat-hatting, what you will. It's not just frivolous. Oh, it's a lot of fun, but flying low has its serious uses. Many times in combat it was necessary to get down on the deck to escape. Or catch someone trying to get away from you. I had always thought so. Incidents in the ETO were proving me right. Big names too. Zemke flew too low, tore up his prop and bellied in. Wound up a POW for the duration. Of course, there was Gentile's famous gaffe. I mean, misjudging a fly-by for the movie cameras. That was dumb. Colonel Blakeslee sent him home for breaking the rules. What Blakeslee should have done was set up a program to train all the pilots in his group in low flying. All fighter pilots for that matter.

The stories of the combat vets at Bartow in combination with how I perceived combat would be, convinced me of the value of flying low under controlled conditions. After I became a Mustang *instructor, I would take all my students out for some "buzzing" practice. I'd take them out over the Gulf or up to the Okefenokee Swamp or down to Lake Okeechobee and tell them, until I see you throwing a rooster tail up, you're not low enough. You had to work these guys because they were afraid to get too low. I would fly off to the side and talk 'em down till the prop was a foot above the weeds.*

They'd get the sight picture and after that it was easy. Not a single one of my forty-nine students hit the ground in combat.

I will admit I sometimes flat-hatted just for the sheer fun of it. The ground personnel at Bottisham were a hard working bunch. They were some real good men. Without them us fly-boys would have been nothing. I really mean that. They didn't get any glory and not much recognition. I had a standing offer that when the opportunity presented itself, I'd do a buzz job just for them. Kind of a thank you. Knew they'd get a kick out of it.

I didn't have a whole lot of airborne aborts, but this day was just like the Rostock mission. During the climb, when the supercharger should have cut in, it didn't. That meant full power would not be available up high. Supercharger and radio failures were probably our two most common reasons for aborting. Both were not any sort of emergency because the airplane would fly back to base just fine. Simply not smart to take into combat.

It was a pretty day and there was no activity back at the base, so I called ops and told them to get the mechs out so I could say thanks. I put Detroit Miss *right down on the grass and headed for the ops building. Pulled up over it and chandelled on to the downwind.*

Got all kinds of compliments from the men afterward. Sergeant Cruikshank, the intell assistant who'd given me my outhouse DFC was at ops and said it was great. Everyone hit the deck when I came over – thought the prop would clip them.

Problem was, Cummins was a real hard nose and my squadron Commanding officer and he was not amused. He really chewed my butt. Especially since I was the squadron safety officer and supposed to know better. He also knew how to get my goat. He grounded me.

I went over to Billy Kemp's quarters. Pounded on his door. When he opened up I waved a bottle of Old Crow *at him and said, "I'm grounded. Let's get out the cards. Play a little poker. Have a drink or two."*

Pretty late in the evening, we hear someone in the hallway yell "Atten-shun!" That just didn't happen in officers' quarters, not at that hour. Colonel Kruzel, the Group CO himself had come over looking for me. He walked in the room and said, "Put that goddam whiskey bottle down. We've got a real deep one tomorrow and you're leading. I want to make sure – not so much that the squadron can find the target, but that everyone can find their way home, and most of our guys can't. So you're leading tomorrow."

"But, Colonel, I'm grounded."

"Well, you've just been un-grounded."

It was an early briefing. A 0330 wake-up meant the mission would be long with a deep penetration into Nazi airspace. When the Intelligence Officer pulled back the curtain at the front of the group briefing room, there was a burst of murmured comment and a couple of louder "Damns." On 7 October, 1944 the red tape stretched deep into Czechoslovakia. The bombers' targets were the Ruckhard and Burks Chemical Plants; vital to the German war effort. The 361st Fighter Group would be escorting B-17s from the 3rd Bomb Division. Takeoff was scheduled for 0630 hours.

Ben Drew was on the board as leading the 375th squadron. One of the squadron pilots said in a stage whisper, "At least we'll know where we're going." Captain Bruce Rowlett, the squadron operations officer, was the deputy leader. Although Ben was a first lieutenant., lead assignments were made based on ability, navigational expertise, and experience, not on rank. The deep penetration would be a tough mission and the odds of encountering the *Luftwaffe* were high.

Major Cummins was sitting in his jeep on the side of the perimeter track as the airplanes taxied out.. Ben gave a big, cheery wave from *Detroit Miss* as he passed by. This did not endear him to the major.

It was a better day than most in England; mostly clear with some scattered low clouds. As I led the squadron to cruising altitude, I thought how good they looked.

Flying my wing were two "Macs". Number two was Second Lieutenant Bob McCandliss. He had 16 missions without "breaking the tape on his guns" as we used to say. He was eager, a good marksman, and an excellent wingman. Number four had engine problems and did not go, so my element leader, Second Lieutenant Bill McCoppin was alone in the third slot.

Bruce, Red, Rowlett was deputy squadron leader and leading the second flight section.

I was sure looking forward to this one. We were on a Ramrod. I loved the Ramrods – after we got the bombers out, we were free to rove and hunt. Going deep into Czechoslovakia also meant one thing for sure – the Luftwaffe *would be up*.

The 375th squadron crossed the English Channel and made landfall in the Netherlands. The fighters closed on the assigned B-17 bomber groups and took up their escort positions. The Third Bomber Division had distinctive red markings on their vertical fins. The markings were a way for the fighter escort to be sure they were with the correct bomber group.

When the squadron was well over Europe, radio conversations told of the groups ahead were being hit by *Me109s* and *FW190s*. Ben's group was clear of enemy fighters, so when he spotted a *staffel* of *Focke-Wulfs* heading for the bomber group flying immediately ahead, he left half the squadron with Rowlett, and took his section to assist. The 190s were already through the bomber group and had split for the deck by the time he caught up. He stayed with that group until their assigned escort returned, then slipped back to his assigned group.

As we approached the targets, the Flak *was heavy and intense. The Jerries had heavy 88 millimeter guns they could shoot like a .22 rifle. I saw them pick off fighters and bombers at 35,000 feet. Bam, one in front. Bam, one behind, and they were bracketed. Bam, and the aircraft would explode in flames. They were good... damn good. They should have been. They had plenty of practice. Lots of targets.*

The heavies on their bomb run had to keep straight and level, holding their altitude and heading. Us fighter pilots considered that part of the flight suicidal. We were always moving all over the sky. Always. We called the bombers "flying coffins". Sitting ducks for those marvelously expert 88 gunners. Of course, I'd also heard the reasoning that your chances of jinking into a shell were just as good as being hit while straight and level. Don't you believe it.

One of our jobs was to count the chutes when a bomber went down. Over the factories, it was, as usual, discouraging. Many times, only one, two, or three chutes would come out. Out of a ten man crew, that meant heavy losses.

The weather was clear and the bombardiers made good runs. Bombing results looked excellent from where I was. Explosions and smoke covered the entire factory complex.

The B-17s made a wide swing to the left and took up their return heading for England. As they cleared the *Flak* concentration around the target, the *Luftwaffe* fighters came at them in strength. Hitting again with all their might. The sky became a tangle of twisting, turning fighters; German and American. Dark trails marked aircraft going down. White contrails showed the criss-crossing paths of opposing airplanes.

The 375th did its job and stayed close to their bomber box. No German fighters had gotten close. A few making head-on attacks were persuaded to break off far out. None of the bombers under the squadron's protection were hit.

Approaching Osnabruck, I recalled it was the same area I had seen the Me 262s three weeks before. I was only the third ever Allied pilot to tangle with a Me 262 and he had made a monkey out of me. I was still trying to figure out what had happened. The jet was fast, so I kept a particularly sharp lookout. Up on one wing. Slide back and up on the other. Keep your head on a swivel. That is the only way for a fighter pilot to fly. Never straight and level. Never.

Ever since getting lost that time back in training, I had concentrated on navigating. Without bragging, I was probably the best fighter navigator in the ETO. I also made a point of listening during briefing. We had been told that Achmer was the home of the Kommando Nowotny, *the first Me262 outfit. I had it marked on my map. I was looking for it. I wanted another crack at the jet wonder-weapon.*

I picked up the Achmer airfield from quite away out. There was a river at one end of the runway which helped me locate it, even from high altitude. I paid particular attention to it while scanning for airplanes high and low.

My diligence paid off. Way down, I saw a pair of 262s taxiing onto the runway. No one else had seen them. I rolled Detroit Miss *on her wingtip and let her nose fall through. Pushed the throttle forward. I hoped my wingmen would be smart enough to follow. They were. Both McCandliss and McCoppin were with me. I was concentrating on the two airplanes on the runway and they'd just have to hang on. I had the power all the way up and the* Merlin *was screaming.*

In the dive, I called the deputy leader, "Redhead, I'm taking my flight down. Two bogies *way low. Two o'clock. You stay with the bombers."*

Airspeed built up fast. 350 mph, 375 mph, 400 mph. I'd only been that fast a few times before. The stick was getting difficult to move. I took a hurried glance behind me. McCandliss was glued to my wing, but I couldn't see McCoppin anywhere.

The dive had started at 15,000 feet and by the time I got down on the deck, I was doing about 450. The controls were as stiff as hell. Part of my brain was worried about the tiny corrections I'd need to shoot well, but mostly I just wanted to get in close. I knew that once the jets had a chance to accelerate, my chances would go way down. I don't think I ever looked anywhere except at those two jets. I leveled just over the tree tops, going like hell. The second 262 had just lifted off and was a straight, no deflection shot. I was closing so fast that over-running was a worry. I waited until he was huge in my windscreen. So close I didn't need the gunsight. I had shot-gunned too many geese, ducks and pheasant to worry about aiming at this range. I pointed my guns at the starboard wing root. I squeezed off a good burst and was right on. He exploded in a tremendous fireball. I went right through the cloud of smoke and debris, swearing at not being able to see the German leader, even for a few seconds. My left wing was thrown up by the violence of the burst. I had to fight to get the wing down and turn for the leader.

The leader was harder to kill. A lot harder. He made a mistake or I never would have got him. It was still a tough shot.

He turned. To this day I don't know why. We all made mistakes in combat. It was the difference between life and death. Sometimes you got away with it, sometimes you didn't. He didn't.

The best I can figure, is he reverted to old habits and turned into his attacker – me. He was in a much faster airplane. If he had kept accelerating straight ahead, he would have outrun me. But that's not the way we thought. When an enemy's nose was pointed at you, you turned. Pulled hard. Harder. Make the bastard overshoot. Spoil his tracking. Increase the deflection. Deflection shooting was the hardest thing to do.

Anyway, he laid the jet over on its side. Going faster each second. It was the toughest shot I ever made. All the months at Bartow, all my previous missions were preparation for that shot. Also, I knew from my earlier – and unsuccessful – encounter with the 262, that I needed lots of lead. Lots of lead.

Now, we were at better than sixty degrees angle off. When he had turned, I turned. My wings must have been close to vertical. I didn't give a damn. I was going to get him. The throttle was through the gate a long time before. Temps must have been way over redline. Didn't know; couldn't look down to check. Didn't care. All I cared about was the yellow pipper-dot. I had it on his fuselage.

The Mustang's controls were stiff. The exertion of flying was tremendous. G's dragged at me. My arms were heavy. I kept grunting – tightening my gut and grunting. The edges of my vision were going gray. Tunnel vision we called it. Didn't care. It was clear in the middle, clear where the pipper was. Clear where he was. I pulled more to get the lead angle.

My advantage was I had airspeed, lots of airspeed. Airspeed equals G. G equals turn. Turn equals lead. I was looking at his planform. He was spread out in front of me. His wingtips grew farther apart. I was closer. Farther until they hit the far rings on my gunsight. He was in range.

I pressed the trigger down and was vaguely aware of shudders as all six fifties began to fire. My bullets were hitting his empennage. I pulled the pipper along his flight path. The flame tracks walked up his fuselage and I could see the high explosive shells twinkling on his fuselage as they hit. I held the trigger down.

Wham, wham. His canopy came off in two chunks. I was close – real close. Tweaked the nose to go over and outside. Set up for a re-attack. Risked a look behind on the other side. A giant ball of smoke laced with flame from the first jet reached up from the ground. Turned back to this one. The Messerschmitt *had flopped over and was spinning inverted. It smashed into the ground.*

Two! I'd gotten both of them.

Air combat is fast and furious, and while time seems to stand still, everything happens in a very short period of time. From the moment I ceased firing, the German anti-aircraft guns opened up and their fire was accurate and wicked. I heard the Flak hitting my fuselage and it rattled like gravel inside a tin can. I pressed the mike button and yelled for McCandliss to join up with me and hit the deck. I wanted to get down to treetop level to avoid the now very heavy and precise Flak. I finally spotted him off to my right. He was burning from nose to tail and wingtip to wingtip. I screamed "Roll and bail, Mac, roll and bail for chrissake."

I did not see whether he bailed out. He was awfully low.

It was time to get the hell clear. I leveled my wings, pushed the nose down, kept my speed up. Reluctantly I checked the engine gages. Pulled the power back before it blew a jug.

I was down on the deck and headed for England, but being fired at from every road intersection, every building, every clump of bushes. There was so much Flak that I called Rowlett and said, "Redhead, I got the two jets, but don't think I can make it home. They are shooting the hell out of me. Please confirm them for me old buddy."

The Flak did let up, but I was taking no chances. I kept jinking and dodging. Used trees for cover. Swerved around any built up area. At the North Sea Coast, the German gunners took their last whack at me with 88's. Including a trick of theirs; throwing shells in front of me hoping I'd hit the column of water from the explosion.

Two! I had gotten two Messerschmitt jets.

Bottisham was a madhouse. Rowlett had radioed ahead that I'd gotten two jets. By the time I got there, most of the group had landed. The stragglers came in after me. There was quite a crowd waiting in Detroit Miss' revetment. Everyone wanted to congratulate me. Which was great, but first I wanted confirmation. I watched as my armorer unscrewed the access plate to get the gun camera film out. He turned to me with the film cartridge in his hand and a long face. He shook his head.

The navy had been using color film in their gun cameras for some time. Uncle Sam's air force was finally catching up. The 361st Group was the first to try it out. On this mission. On selected airplanes. Not one Group, squadron or flight leader's film worked that day. Not one. The cartridges were enough different that they all jammed.

My number three man, McCoppin, had made it back. Without a scratch.

He was in the debriefing room when I got there. He hadn't seen a thing. He said he'd seen a Flak site off to the side and swung out to strafe it. Then he'd gone around the Flak that was hosing me and come home alone.

I did not have official confirmation. At Bottisham, everyone acted like I had gotten them and hoped for the best. Amid the celebrating I sure wished I knew what had happened to Bobby McCandliss. It was worse over the next weeks. Every time I saw the initials MIA, Missing In Action, after his name, I wondered.

Within a couple days, after the official combat action reports from the debriefing had gone up to 8th Air Force HQ, confirmation was granted by General Doolittle himself.

At the time, I guessed he may have done it for morale purposes. The 262 had gotten quite a reputation as unbeatable and he wanted to let everyone in the Eighth to know that the jets were vulnerable. Mine weren't the first ones shot down, but I was the first to get full credit. The earlier ones were shared kills.

His action made me officially an ace. Both by 8th AF standards and the more traditional five in the air.

Years later, I suspect that General Doolittle knew the jets were down because of information he was given from Ultra decrypts of encoded Luftwaffe radio messages. He was on the small list of top leaders who had access to that top secret information. He never admitted this to me in subsequent meetings after the war, but, by then, he did not have to.

Sergeant Cruikshank of the 275 Squadron Intelligence Branch shows Lieutenant Drew the paperwork on his double victory.

28

RHEINE

Wingman Down

Bob McCandliss had followed Ben Drew all the way down in the high speed dive. Some other pilot had named the airplane he was in, "Hitler's Nemesis". An odd quirk of the P-51B was that its thin wing was less susceptible to compressibility and the razorback canopy caused less turbulence. The B was easier to fly at high speeds than the newer D's.

He was behind and slightly to the right of *Detroit Miss* when the first jet exploded. When Ben went into the steep turn to catch the second *Messerschmitt*, McCandliss cut to the inside to get closer to his leader. It worked too well. He watched the pilot bail out of the second jet and had to pull up to avoid tangling in the *Luftwaffe* pilot's parachute. He was close enough to see the parachute canopy was a patchwork of grey, white, and brown cloth. It looked like several used chutes had been stitched together for one good canopy. If he had been seconds earlier, he would have hit the spinning jet. He did get bumped by the fireball of its crash.

Anti-aircraft fire was intense. The *Luftwaffe* had put guns everywhere. The heavy 88's may have been too big to track low fast targets, but the other weapons did not have that problem.

McCandliss would have gone on to join Ben and get out of there, except he looked off to one side and noticed a flexible mount gun, less than 200 yards away, firing while leading him like a skeet shooter. He lost his temper and took it out on a single, heavy machine gun ahead of him in an open field. The long barrel stuck out between slabs of armor plate. The gun was slightly off dead center and he was too low to bank, so he pressed rudder to skid his *Mustang* on target. A dirt road with a wooden post, wire fence went under his propeller. Lurid purple-red fire balls floated and grew from the gun. His own bullets kicked up dirt and sparkled on the steel plate. One of the flaming balls went into his left wing. It punched through the fuel tank, out the trailing edge and turned the P-51 into a blowtorch. More shrapnel took a chunk out of his bulged *Malcolm* canopy. He started to climb.

Thinking an empty gas tank would not burn, he moved the fuel selector. His engine coughed. The fire did not go out. He switched back.

The hole over his head created a huge draft which sucked flames and smoke into the cockpit. His left ankle was in flames. He knew he had to get out. Normal emergency bailout was to roll the airplane over, but he did not know how high he was because of the blinding smoke.

McCandliss yanked his oxygen hose free, pulled the clasp and released lap belt and shoulder harness. He did not chop the throttle. He did not re-trim. He jettisoned what was left of the canopy. As he jumped, turbulence whipped the canvas seat straps around his right ankle. The straps kept his foot inside. The canopy edge cut into his calf. He was trapped against the fuselage. The slipstream held his arms over his head. He kicked. Kicked harder. Again and again. The airplane nosed up until it stalled and began a violent, power-on spin. Air buffeted his body. He kicked. He kicked until exhausted.

Bob McCandliss began to wonder what it would be like to hit the ground. He had time to imagine what the impact would be like. He pictured his wife. He could see her face. He had met Virginia Goodall in Tallahassee – at the Women's College. They married three weeks later. She had nursed him through his pneumonia. Was with him in training at Dale Mawbrey Field. She was going to have their baby. Would it be a boy or a girl? Perhaps a girl as pretty as his wife. He saw her face. He kicked. He came free.

The back of his left knee slammed into the horizontal stabilizer. He tumbled away. Found the D-ring. Put left hand over right and pulled. The white nylon opened bosomy and soft. In one swing he hit the ground. He missed the high tension electrical wires on either side. Had a quick glimpse of a canal to the west.

The airplane crashed in a plowed field two hundred yards from where McCandliss landed. It kept burning.

He had come down through a tree. He was on the ground, but the parachute was snagged on the branches. He struggled trying to pull it down for a few minutes, but decided it wasn't worth the effort. People were headed for the burning wreck of the airplane. McCandliss took off his *Mae West* and stuffed it in a hole between the tree roots and headed away from the crowd – toward the canal in the hope it was in Holland.

He was gimping across an open, grassy field as fast as his injured legs would allow, when he heard a pistol shot at his back. He stopped. Put his hands up. Sat down.

Two men came up to him. One was in civilian clothes with heavy boots. The other wore the grey trousers and close necked uniform of the *Luftwaffe*. He had his personal Walther pistol in his hand. His rank badges showed he was a *Leutnant*. The civilian was Dutch and cradled a shotgun.

The curious crowd around the airplane edged closer until the fifty caliber ammunition started to explode. Several noticed McCandliss and his captors and came across the field. McCandliss carried a gun because of stories of allied fighter pilots being lynched before the proper authorities could get to them. He was relieved that his captor was in uniform and armed.

They had him get up and went back to the tree he had landed in. With several people helping, the parachute was pulled down. His Colt 45, the six clips of bullets he had in various pockets, and his homemade ammo belt were taken from him. He wore a large hunting knife strapped to his leg, but it was gone. Lost in the bailout. Also in his pockets were candy bars, a bottle of pepper, and a first aid kit.

He was asked if he was hurt. He nodded his head. Said, "Yes, *Ja-Ja*, yes, *Oui*, Yes I am hurt."

The field bandage from his first aid kit and the dressing from the German officer's were enough to cover the burned area on McCandliss' left leg. The smashed muscles in his other leg were not visible. His white scarf was stained with fresh blood. He removed it and found a sharp chunk of plastic from his canopy. The layers of cloth had saved his neck from a severe cut. They gave him the parachute to carry.

There was a hunting lodge in the trees McCandliss had not noticed before. He guessed that the *Leutnant* was probably on leave and doing some sport hunting. He was lucky the *Luftwaffe* officer was there, as the crowd seemed hostile.

A *Volkswagen* was parked near the lodge. The *Leutnant* indicated they were going to use it. To get to the car, McCandliss had to climb over a fence. He was awkward hugging the voluminous chute like a bale of laundry. When he stepped down on the other side, the pain began. He had not felt any until then, but now his burns scorched, his battered legs spiked with pain, his neck ached, every muscle in his body hurt. He felt like the losing team after a football game – enough pain for all eleven men. He stumbled into the small, beetle-shaped automobile that would be so familiar twenty years later. The *Leutnant* drove him to the Wetteringen town jail.

A normally large room had been divided into cells with lumber frames covered with chicken wire. He was put into an end cell with a bunk. There was graffiti by other prisoners on the walls and wood. One was, "*Un move' souvenir des n'escapade.*" McCandliss knew enough French to translate, "In bad memory of an reckless prank." It was not an encouraging thought.

He collapsed on the bunk, exhausted. Nightmares of burning and falling disturbed his rest.

Four hours later a big *Wehrmacht* lorry with armed guards took him to the Rheine Airfield where he had been shot down. It was a tedious, cautious journey. The soldiers were afraid of prowling American fighters. In the *VW* it had taken five minutes. The *SkF* truck took an hour.

McCandliss was lead into a room in the airfield's operations building. A *Luftwaffe* Major stood behind a table. Everything taken from McCandliss was spread out in front of him. He smiled at McCandliss. Picked up the standard American issue 45 pistol. In six swift moves, he field stripped it and laid the parts down neatly. He smiled at his prisoner again. Picked up the frame and equally swiftly, reassembled the pistol. In English, he said, "This is a pretty good gun."

He walked around the table and began asking questions. The answer he got to them all was, "McCandliss, Robert K., Second Lieutenant, United States Army Air Force, 704693." The major seemed bored and soon had McCandliss taken upstairs to a small cell. A guard brought him food. He could not stomach the coarse *schwarzbrot*, black bread, but enjoyed the lentil soup. He stayed there overnight.

McCandliss awoke feeling better. His legs still hurt, but the shock had worn off and he managed to eat some jam and *schwarzbrot*. The jam was cloying and sticky; the bread gritty and tasted like pine, but it was solid food. He was handed a brown paper sack by a guard who waved his hands indicating he would be leaving the cell. Nothing happened for an hour.

A stocky German soldier unlocked and walked into the cell. He had on a grey uniform with baggy pants tucked into black, hobnailed boots. The tabs on his shoulders were mostly cloth with a thin surround of piping. McCandliss knew he was not a sergeant or a private, so assumed he was a *Gefreiter*, a corporal.

"*Guten Tag*," his voice was high pitched for his barrel chest and thick neck, "*kommen Sie mit*." He used his hands to show he wanted McCandliss to stand and go with him. "*Können Sie Deutsch sprechen?*" McCandliss shook his head no.

The corporal had left his rifle leaning against the wall outside the cell. He slung it and a grey fabric pack over his shoulder and lead McCandliss down the corridor and down stairs. Outside a truck was waiting to take them to the train. He forgot to take his paper sack. He should have; it contained food for the trip to Frankfurt.

By late 1944, the German trains rarely went through towns or cities. Most railroad yards, even little ones with only a spur or two, had been bombed out. The usual procedure was for the train to stop in a secluded spot outside town, the passengers would get off and walk to the other side of the town and get on another train for the trip to the next town. It made for slow travel. For McCandliss it was an advantage. He became very stiff if he sat for any length of time and the walks stretched his muscles. He estimated he walked ten to fifteen miles each day. His walk was erratic. Besides his injuries, the sole of his flying boot had been torn off escaping the airplane.

The truck dropped them off in the countryside. To reach the train, they had to walk through an apple orchard. The apples were ripe and red. They both picked handfuls and shoved them in their pockets. They were all McCandliss ate for the next three days.

The corporal guard was a stolid type in his thirties. Either he thought it unlikely his prisoner could escape because they were deep in Germany or he was too dull to see the stupid mistakes he made. The pall of being a prisoner in a strange, enemy land did not keep McCandliss from being amused by his fumbling guard.

It was dark and late when, for a change, the train pulled into an urban station. They and many of the passengers got off and took a break on the platform. Suddenly his guard said something about "*le Pissoir*" and ran off to find the bathroom. More likely he needed more than a urinal because of so many apples, but he knew McCandliss would understand the French term. The trip had become easier with the realization that guard and prisoner both spoke some French. McCandliss nodded and kept pacing in a circle to keep limber. Time stretched. McCandliss realized he was alone on the platform and the guard had left his rifle resting against an oil drum. He paced some more. Thought about making a break for it. Decided it was too risky in a flying suit in an unknown city with a lynch minded populace. He looked up and down the platform. No one was in sight. He brushed up a palm full of sand and grit from the pavement. Dumped it down the barrel of the rifle. The guard returned in minutes hitching his trousers. They got back on the train.

Mainz is a beautiful old city on the Rhein River. The guard had a friend he wanted to visit there and dragged McCandliss along. Walking through the twisting streets of the older section, the guard was eager and walked briskly. McCandliss' legs slowed him down. His guard never noticed and was soon out of sight around a bend. McCandliss stopped for a breath and looked around. A little old man rushed from his front porch and began beating him with a stout piece of lumber, screaming in German the whole time. At first, McCandliss was so surprised he took a couple of good whacks, but then tried to fend off the blows. The old guy kept swinging so McCandliss took off in a gimpy run. He caught up with, and stayed beside, his guard for the next blocks. The guard never realized he had been gone. His friend was not home. The next train took them to Frankfurt.

Usually, because he was a prisoner, McCandliss was last to get a seat and stood if the train was crowded.

She had a pretty face with blue eyes. Maybe twenty years old. She caught McCandliss' eye. Smiled shyly. He barely had the strength to smile back. She asked the corporal guard if he was wounded. The guard said, "*Ja, er ist verwundet.*" She got up and gave the foreigner her seat. She stood until they had to get off for the next town.

A grey, sodden overcast hung over the Frankfurt railroad yard. The train was at the end of the yard, near a forest and stretch of highway. 88 millimeter guns were scattered all around, muzzles pointed skyward, sweeping left and right, up and down. Air raid sirens began their banshee wail. The passengers panicked and rushed out of the multiple doors on the side of the coach cars. They ran into the forest to hide. All of them including the guard. Who forgot his rifle again.

McCandliss sat in the empty compartment, staring at the rifle, looking outside. He knew the clouds were too low for fighters to come down and strafe. He was happy to stay where he was with a roof over his head to avoid the drizzle and spent *flak* shrapnel falling from the sky. The Germans were terrified of strafing. Rightfully so, he thought. He had seen dozens of railroad boxcars and coaches with bullet holes all the way through. High on one side, low on the other. He looked at the wood veneer wall of the compartment. He looked at the open door on the other side. If some crazy pilot did get below the overcast.... He got up and slowly stepped down from the train and wandered to the woods to find his guard.

The attack never came. After half an hour shuffling in the deep, soft pine straw, the passengers heard the all clear and went back to the train. Corporal guard could not find the compartment they had been in. The compartment he had left his rifle in.

The guard walked along the side of the cars, plaintively asking, "Is this where the American was riding?" A low wooden box covering wires and cables stuck out from the gray gravel of the road bed to a switch-signal box. The guard tripped on it and fell on his face. McCandliss caught him by his great coat and stood him up.

So busy was the guard looking up through the windows, that six feet later he fell again. Passengers were watching now as McCandliss again hauled his captor to his feet. An old man shook his head.

The search continued. A short conversation with two women. The guard walked farther. Another cable box, another stumble forward.

McCandliss grabbed but missed. His guard sprawled on dirt and cinders. The crowd of passengers laughed. McCandliss laughed too. This was not what he anticipated being a prisoner would be like.

When, at last, they found the compartment... and rifle, McCandliss was surprised when his corporal lead him back off the train. In fractured French, he explained something about the tracks ahead being blown up – they were better off on their own.

Two hundred yards through the forest there was a road of well packed dirt covered with pine needles. The corporal waved down a passing truck, spoke with the driver. The pair climbed the tailgate into the canvas covered back. The heavy *SkF* ground into gear and started off. They sat on green painted wooden crates and could see out through the rolled up canvas sides and front.

The forest was old. Trees reached up a hundred feet or more. There was little undergrowth and the leafy floor neat looking. An airplane appeared off to one side. Then another, and another. Fighters. A mix of round engined *Focke-Wulf 190s* and long engined *Me 109s* with black prop spinners and a bulge on the top of the cowling – G models. The fighters were carefully placed so no trees appeared to have been removed. Leafy branches and pine boughs had been laid over most wings, canopies and fuselages. There were men in black coveralls working on some. Most of the airplanes sat alone, leaf green, spruce grey, part of the shadowed woods like hidden dragons of a Grimm fairy tale.

McCandliss knew how to fly airplanes. Air Force Intelligence had shown the pilots of his group photographs of German cockpits, had briefed them on basic switchology, operating procedures. He could steal a 190 or 109 and fly it to England. He would be a hero. Famous. He would be on his way home instead of some far off prison camp. He dreamt about stealing a current *Luftwaffe* fighter as the truck lurched along what he now thought of as a taxiway, not a road. It was a pleasant thought, if an unlikely one. Sunlight glared as they drove onto a large field that was the runways for the fighters hidden in the forest.

Robert McCandliss' Prisoner-of-war identification.
The original was printed on orange paper.

The truck let them off near a two story, concrete building that was the operations center for the dispersed *Geschwader*. His guard, whom McCandliss had taken to thinking of as the "Yokel Corporal," went straight up the front steps, down the main hall into a large room with rows of seats facing a wall covered with large maps, slate boards with words stencil-painted on, blank squares for chalked in names, numbers, frequencies. They were in the *Geschwader's* main briefing room. *Yokel Corporal* wandered about looking for someone to take his prisoner from him. McCandliss went to the front row of wooden chairs and stood staring. Line diagrams and unit designations were on the board.

The *Luftwaffe* defense network was laid out for him. He studied the numbers, the names. Methodically, he memorized the data. It would be valuable intell when he got back.... if he got back.

An officer in a black leather *Luftwaffe* flying jacket walked in. The corporal moved to a position of attention. He moved slowly, as always. His eyes were locked straight ahead. The German pilot stared at McCandliss. McCandliss stared back. The German knew. Here was another fighter pilot. A man like himself. A man he could have met in the sky. An enemy. Here in his briefing room. "*Soldat! Gehen sie 'raus. Schnell. Dummkopf.*"

Yokel Corporal answered, "*Jawohl, Herr Hauptmann,*" in his peculiar squeaky voice and took McCandliss by the arm. The *Luftwaffe* Captain walked behind and pushed them out the door. Told the corporal to go to the car waiting outside.

Their transportation was a 1934 model Chevrolet coupe. The Chevy had been fitted with an awkward looking charcoal burner which stuck up like a whiskey still out of the lidless trunk. The doors were locked and the windows open. *Yokel* guard tugged on the door handles. Tried both on that side. Tugged again and looked puzzled. McCandliss reached in and pulled up the door lock. Opened the door for his guard. He was having trouble not laughing.

At the *Dulag-Luft*, the holding unit for the larger *Stalag*, his companion and guard, the *yokel-corporal*, left him. He did not say goodbye. He turned and ambled away as stolid as ever. Off to his next assignment.

McCandliss was given a short interrogation. He stuck to the basic rule of name, rank, serial number only. Even when the *Luftwaffe* officer told him that most of his crew had been killed, but the survivors had been captured, and talked, so McCandliss might as well tell him everything. "My crew?" thought McCandliss, "In a *Mustang*?" He kept his mouth shut.

He was put in a cell. The cell was ten feet by six feet. There was a window at one end and an electric heater suspended from the ceiling. A steel door with a peephole at the other side. To go to the bathroom, he pulled on a lever and a guard would escort him down the hallway to the latrine. He would drink lots of water so he had to go frequently and get out of his cell. He was all alone. He had no one to talk to. No one to support him, help him.

Second Lieutenant Robert K. McCandliss, 704693, spent three long weeks in solitary confinement.

29

ACHMER II

Misfortunes

The last quarter of 1944 was a confusing time for Georg-Peter Eder – for all the pilots flying the *Messerschmitt 262*. Unit names changed fast to reflect political maneuvering. Pilots and support people moved from base to base; sometimes with the same unit, sometimes with a newly named one. The fighter *Schwalbe*, the *schnellbomber Sturmvogel* had many maintenance problems and unforeseen glitches. Parts and jet fuel were in short supply. Administration, record keeping were a paperwork mess. Everything was rushed. Through the chaos, the pilots had but one goal – they would fly the world's most advanced airplane against their enemies. Ready or not. Operational losses, bureaucratic bungling meant nothing. Put us in a cockpit. Let us fly. Let us do our best to defend the Fatherland against the invaders.

Oberleutnant Eder had been assigned to an Me 262 outfit as he had requested. His experience against heavy bombers was needed for the new jet. His initial assignment was to III/EJG2 based at Lechfeld. However, the Experimental Jet Fighter Group, *Erprobungs-JagdGeschwader*, suffered from all the problems associated with the Me 262 program. Little flight training was possible because priority had been shifted to the newly formed Jet *Kommando* at Achmer Airfield.

Achmer was near the Dutch border and under the bomber tracks in and out of the *Reich*. The short range of the jets would not be a problem—their targets, the bombers, would come to them. The *Kommando* was headed by the spectacularly successful national celebrity, Walter Nowotny. Nowotny was a newly promoted Major with 256 kills. He had been awarded Diamonds, Swords and Oak leaves to his Knight's Cross – the highest award in Germany. General of Fighters Galland hoped that his appointment would create the publicity needed to boost the jet fighter program. At the time of his appointment, Nowotny was twenty-three years old.

Kommando Nowotny was loaded with likely candidates for rapid success in the *Messerschmitt 262*. They came from all fronts, from many types of fighters. The bulk of the selected pilots arrived in Achmer on 2 and 3 October. Most of them had not yet flown the *Me 262*. While they were being trained as rapidly as possible, preparations went forward for the *Kommando's* first combat operation. That mission was to take place on 7 October.

Eder had begun training with a cockpit checkout and engine starts instructed by *Oberingenieur* Leuther. He was not ready for the first go and watched events from near the hangar with other spectating pilots and ground crews.

There had been no warning of the attack. The local warning radar had picked up blips, but the *Mustangs'* dive had been so steep that their progress over the ground seemed to be normal cruise speed. There was no correlation with their rapid descent. The first the watchers knew of the enemy fighters was their appearance over the trees off the runway end. Belated alarms rang and howled over the base. The *Flak* gunners looked away from the departing jets. Swung barrels toward targets. Began shooting at the Americans.

Distinctive pulsed smoke came from the lead *Mustang's* guns, a sparkle of shell casings came out of the chutes. The number two *Messerschmitt* was flown by *Leutnant* Kobert. It exploded in a ball of fire and black smoke. Kobert was killed in the explosion. The *Mustang* flew through the cloud of debris.

All eyes shifted to *Oberleutnant* Bley in the lead *Me262*. He was moving away, but high enough that those on the ground could watch the action. Eder and other single-seat fighter pilots, were surprised to see Bley bank the jet and go into a sweeping left turn. He had been accelerating and would have out run the *Mustang* if he had kept going straight ahead. However, Bley was a Me 110 pilot. A standard survival tactic used by *Zerstörer* pilots when attacked by a faster airplane was to turn into an attacker and cause him to overshoot. Usually it worked. This time the turn gave the attacking P-51 the chance to use geometry to cut inside and close the range. Bley's reaction was natural for a 110 pilot, but fatal.

Back at the airfield, they could not see the bullets walking up the fuselage toward the cockpit, but they did see parts of the canopy blow off as the *Schwalbe* flipped onto its back and spun inverted. Somehow Bley jumped and opened his parachute.

The second *Mustang* had closely followed and had to pop-up to avoid hitting Bley on his short descent. The *Mustang* turned right to keep up with his leader. He was far away, near the airfield at Rheine, when the crowd saw it burst into flames from nose to tail. It started to climb. Fighter pilot eyes had a brief glimpse of a parachute and a spinning airplane.

On the Achmer runway, another Me 262 lay awkwardly off to one side. *Oberfähnreich* Russel was at high speed on his takeoff roll when the spent brass casings from the *Mustang's* guns rained down in front of him. One, or more, were at a freak angle when the weak, artificial rubber tires ran over them. Both main wheels blew out. Sparks flew as the hubs ground down. The main landing gear legs collapsed. So did the nose gear. The *Messerschmitt* slid along on its engine pods. Dirt and debris hit the spinning compressor blades. Both engines were ruined.

Russel was uninjured and soon out of the cockpit swearing at his bad luck.

The fourth *Messerschmitt* managed to avoid Russel's aircraft and got successfully airborne. However, later, its long, thin nose strut snapped on landing and it too wound up off the side of the runway.

Two *Schwalbe* from the satellite airfield at Hesepe had better luck. They bagged a pair of P-51s and returned safely.

Later, Eder would comment, "That attack was a terrible blow. Here we'd trained and trained; finally going out in unit strength and this *Mustang* shoots the first two out of the sky. It was a terrible blow to morale.

"And that was not the end of the disasters."

There were days with no flying while damage was repaired and more jets brought on-line. Eder's instructor, Leuther, was to fly a test flight on a repaired *Messerschmitt 262*. He had Eder and a couple other pilots he had been working with come out to watch. Perhaps he rushed because of the audience. Perhaps he mis-estimated the wind. Perhaps he did not know the capabilities of his new airplane. Whatever the reason, Leuther tried to take-off with a tailwind.

He ran out of runway before he had enough airspeed to fly. He tried to snatch the 12,000 pound airplane off the ground. The 262's nose came up, the entire aircraft shuddered, fell off on a wing, the tip dug in, it cartwheeled, burst into flame, smashed into the maintenance hangar. Leuther was dead. Five new Me 262s destroyed. A dozen mechanics, killed or hospitalized. Their factory training and field experience with the complex *Schwalbe* more of a loss to the program than the destruction of the airplanes themselves.

The demands on the pilots of the *Kommando Nowotny* were relentless. It was vital that the *Schwalbe* be a success. *Oberleutnant* Bley was back at work the day after he was shot down; limping on a ankle twisted on his parachute landing. He was in the air again as soon as there were airplanes to fly. He was, after all, the CO of the Second *Staffel*. He had an example to set. Bley had eight official victories while flying the *Me110*. On one remarkable mission, he had shot down four P-38 *Lightnings*. He wanted more.

On the 28 of October, Eder was waiting in line for take-off when Bley as the *staffel* leader went first.

"I do not think his engines were quite right. But he never said anything on the radio. Not that he would have. They had to be really bad before we would not fly. Bley taxied into position, released the brakes and started to roll. He was not accelerating right, for each second the airspeed did not increase as it should. It was nightmarish, it was so slow. I could tell he was not getting sufficient speed to fly, he must have realized it too. Puffs of grey smoke came out of his exhausts – there was not full power. Maybe he thought he could hold it up through sheer skill. Maybe… He tried. The nose lifted. Took forever for the wheels to come off the pavement. He raised the gear right away. He held meters above what little runway remained. I found myself shouting for him to fly, pushing hard on my pedals, lifting my ass off the seat.

"There were some pilings in the river off the end of the runway. They didn't stick up far, but it was enough. They reached up for him. Reached up and gutted his *Messerschmitt* like a fish.

"I was scheduled to be the CO of *Staffel* 3 of the *Kommando*. Instead I took over as *Kapitain* of 2 *Staffel* after Bley was killed. The third *Staffel* was never formed.

"That CO tour didn't last very long either; only until the next tragic accident."

A pair of VIP's visited Achmer on 8 November. General Keller, the commander of *Luftwaffe* bombers, and General Galland, the fighter commander.

On his second attempt of the day, Major Nowotny took-off on his first combat mission in a *Me262*. It was to be his only mission.

Exactly what happened will never be known. Nowotny apparently shot down an American *Mustang*, but soon afterwards called in on the radio to say he was having difficulties. It is uncertain whether he was on fire from battle damage or one of the unreliable *Jumo* engines had blown up.

Eder was outside with Galland and Keller waiting for Nowotny to return when a *Schwalbe* came down through the clouds and plunged into the ground. Walter Nowotny was dead in the wreckage. The watchers were stunned.

Galland told Eder he was now commander of the *kommando*. It was to be a short assignment.

The next day, Eder flew and claimed two P-51s downed. His promotion to *Hauptmann* came the day after that.

On 11 November, the majority of *Kommando* Nowotny joined III/EJ2. Most of the pilots went to Lechfeld for more training. Georg-Peter Eder had been the commanding officer of the first operational jet fighter unit for four days.

On the day of the transfer, Eder claimed two B-17s and another P-51 destroyed. It was a confusing time. According to surviving records Eder got the only official unit victory in November of 1944. His claims and those of many other *Luftwaffe* pilots in late 1944 and 1945 were never confirmed. If they had been, Georg-Peter Eder would probably be the top scorer in the *Me262*. French records credit Eder with 25 kills in the *Me262*.

As it was, the now *Hauptmann* Eder's first official kill in the *262* was an interesting one. He attacked an American reconnaissance *Lightning* on the thirteenth, his favorite number, and, while checking his armament switches, rammed it. The *Me262* was so fast that even experienced pilots had trouble adjusting to its speed. His *Schwalbe* was unaffected and Eder returned to base safely. The kill was confirmed by the crash of a P-38 near Schleissheim at the right time and date.

Eder flew the *Messerschmitt 262* as frequently as possible. All the *Schwalbe* pilots did. It was not very often.

Me 262 under tow. The cables to the main gear were to take some of the strain off the Schwalbe's notoriously weak nose gear strut

30

GOUROCK

Homeward Bound

Ben Drew flew more missions after Achmer, but as much as combat can be called routine, these last missions were routine. On what would be his next to last mission, he saw two 109s in the far distance. They did not come close.

He flew his last mission from England on the First of November, 1944; a four hour and 15 minute long "Ramrod" to Gelsenkirchen. Coincidentally, the Gelsenkirchen mission was also the last for Lieutenant Colonel Kruzel and Red Rowlett.

To his frustration, the next day was the best of the war for all of Fighter Command: 175 German aircraft were destroyed. The 361st Group accounting for nine of them. Sadly, the 375th lost two pilots; Lieutenant Narvis, who had flown with Ben, was MIA, and Lieutenant Charles Moore.

Getting out of England was much slower than his arrival there, but pilots going home had a much different priority than those going to war. First, they spent days hanging around Little Walden while orders were cut, multiple pieces of paper signed or initialed, travel arranged. Eventually, the three of them rode a bus to the Replacement Center at Chorley. They spent more days there before going on to Gourock in

Scotland. In the port city, they waited again. This time for a ship which would take them back to the United States.

Joe Kruzel wore a thin mustache and had wrinkles around his eyes. The wrinkles may have been from squinting toward the sun or laugh lines – either was appropriate. Kruzel was a veteran. He had fought the Japanese. He had fought the Germans. Now he was done and on his way home. He sat in front of one of three desks crammed in the small office. His legs were stretched out with his feet resting on a folding chair. Ben Drew was behind the desk with a page of penciled notes and phone numbers in front of him. He was not smiling. Across the room, Rowlett was using the heavy, black telephone on another desk. He was speaking loudly and slowly in an attempt to be understood over a poor connection. He was not smiling either. Kruzel was smiling when he was not softly whistling *My Bonny Lies Over the Ocean.*

News of the German surprise advance in the Ardennes had come in the previous day. The seriousness of the situation was reported in *Stars and Stripes,* local newspapers and over the BBC radio. A quarter of a million German troops were advancing. The two young pilots wanted to get back in the action. They thought they would be needed desperately. Ben and *Redhead* were calling anyone they could think of who might help them get back to their squadron. Get back to any squadron. So far, every time they talked to someone who could make a decision they got the same answer; they were not needed –desperately or otherwise. Go home. With every rebuff, the wiser Kruzel would nod his head, chuckle, and say, "I told you so. Might as well relax and enjoy what you got coming. You boys deserve to go home."

Rowlett hung up the telephone and shook his head. Early the next morning they were on their way across the Atlantic.

Lieutenant Colonel Joe Kruzel.
Deputy, then Commander of 361st Fighter Group.
Ace with both Japanese and German kills.

Bill Kemp was not ready to go home. His stay in the hospital after being wounded kept him from flying the required combat hours at the same time his buddy Drew did. In addition he had volunteered for a second tour with the 375th so when he did go back to Illinois it was only for a month's leave before returning and resuming the lead of D flight. He was with the 361st Group when they moved from Little Walden to Chievres in Belgium. In his remaining missions, Kemp did not shoot down any more airplanes.

Their final score was a tie – by whichever accounting was used. According to Eighth Air Force official records, each had destroyed seven enemy airplanes; one on the ground and six in the air. The air kills made them six plane aces by the traditional count. As for the *Katzenjammer Kids'* private score board, it was two and two.

Drew granted Kemp credit for the last one on the day of his "triple". The first two were, he said, "easy shots, couldn't miss, but that last *Jerry* put up a fight down in the weeds." His other credit was for the *Focke-wulf* he shot down at Chartres. Ben explained, "I was right next to you and knew what a brawl that was."

Kemp ceded Drew the Me 109 near Rostock, "That amount of hard work is worth something.", and the slow, straight and level, old *Heinkel* bomber, "There were 300 fighters up there and you were the only one who saw the bastard."

THE KATZENJAMMER ACES: DREW and KEMP
A PR shot taken after Achmer; Ben's final score is in victory flags on the canopy of *Detroit Miss*.

In a photograph taken after his success at Achmer, Ben Drew is helped onto Detroit Miss by Sergeant Vern Richards who created the elaborate kill markings based on the German naval flag.

31

FRöHLICHE WEIHNACHTEN

Christmas 1944

The winter of 1944 was cold and snowy. More so than in most years. Nature seemed to object to the violence of the war and make life as difficult as possible for both sides. However, the miserable weather worked to the German's advantage in mid-December. Before dawn on the thirteenth, batteries of searchlights lit the bottoms of the solid, low cloud layer. The reflected light illuminated the American lines for the German gunners. The *Wehrmacht* 7th *armee* and the 5th and 6th *Panzer armee* under the command of *Feldmarschall* Walther Model attacked through the rugged terrain of the Ardennes. They brought up all available reserve forces with the aim of retaking the port of Antwerp and splitting the American and British armies. Within days the German army drove over thirty miles into Belgium and Luxembourg. The salient was called "The Bulge".

Luftwaffe airpower was originally part of the plan, but low ceilings and poor visibility kept planes on the ground. Weather kept Allied aircraft on the ground as well. When the clouds cleared after more than two weeks, American and British fighters and bombers rolled to the attack and the Germans began a retreat.

The snow stayed on the ground during the clear cold days.

Georg-Peter Eder had been promoted to Major. In the continuing confusion of *Me262* assignments, he was now commanding 9 *Staffel* of JG-7. The *Staffel* was being moved to Parchim in the Mecklenberg midway between Hamburg and Berlin. Eder was in the midst of the classic aviation CO's dilemma; he was trying to fly missions while running his unit. He had gotten airborne often enough to claim forty P-47 *Thunderbolts* destroyed on the ground during the Ardennes campaign, but as Christmas approached, concerns with transport, parts, fueling, quarters for his men, and the incredible minutiae of moving were taking more and more of his time.

The *Staffel* had less than half its allotted pilots. Everyone was working hard. There was no leave to go home for anyone. Even those who had family nearby in Ludwigslust or Schwerin. December 25 might have been just another day except Eder invited all his pilots to the local inn. All of them; officer and enlisted. Even the very junior enlisted. The *Luftwaffe* was not the same one he had joined in 1939. Such fraternization would have been unheard of then. However, back then, there also would have been many cases of brandy and German sparkling wine, *sekt*, instead of the paltry half dozen bottles they had scrounged.

The spirit of the holiday remained. Three of his youngest pilots, all teenagers, had gone into the nearest pine grove and brought back a small tree. All the pilots pitched in to decorate it with colored paper chains and shiny strips of aluminum the RAF bombers threw out as defensive chaff. They topped their tree with a star cut from a tin can. As *Staffel Kapitain*, Eder said a few words. They sang favorite carols and poured what *Sekt* they had. They drank from a motley collection of glasses and mugs which made a variety of tings and tunks when they touched edges as they wished each other, "*Fröhliche Weihnachten*", "Merry Christmas."

*   *   *

Winter for the men at the *StalagLuft* in Barth was better thanks to Bob McCandliss. He had been called a tinkerer since he was a child and now he found himself literally one of the camp tinkers. He was a professional tin smith. His fellow prisoners bought his wares not for cash, but barter or the exchange medium of the camps – cigarettes.

Red Cross parcels included cans of powdered milk, instant coffee, jam. The cans were his raw material. Each hut had a stove for heat and cooking. The cooking pans and pots were made from flattened and reshaped tin cans. Very little solder could be retrieved from the cans, so sections were jointed together. The seam was unsealed, but one cooking, especially of something sugary, caulked the seam nicely. McCandliss worked out a better joint that used less metal and was stronger. But his best invention was an oven made out of tin cans. The *Mac-Oven* sat on top of the stove, the hot air went into an outer chamber and then out into the normal stove pipe. The inner chamber was good for baking potatoes, crude bread, and pies of fruit with cracker crusts. Best of all, the additional surfaces and circulation heated the room more efficiently. Barth was on a peninsula jutting into the Baltic Sea so warmth was valuable.

McCandliss had made himself a mallet out of thick boards swiped from under a hut. Through the camp scrounger, he had a triangular file from a bribed guard. He used it to make "Chinese" style saws out of packing bands. Crude pliers, tinsnips, a knife, and a heavy lag bolt with a question mark shaped end were also in his tool kit.

One day, a truck filled with Russian prisoners drove by. As they passed, McCandliss crossed the bent bolt with his mallet to form the symbol of the Communist Party. The prisoners cheered and waved.

McCandliss tried to stay busy. He built ovens. He wrote letters. He made pots and pans. He wrote more letters. He walked. He exercised his battered legs. He tried not to worry while he waited for mail. While he hoped and waited for the answer to the biggest question in his life.

Virginia McCandliss was pregnant when he had left for England. The baby had been due soon after he was shot down. Finally, a letter arrived. In it his wife told him how well she and the baby were doing. How cute the baby was. That the baby was growing fast. How much she and the baby missed him. He read and reread the letter, looking for a hint. No where had Virginia said whether the baby was a boy or a girl.

McCandliss played the flute in the all POW camp symphony orchestra. The music was one more thing to keep him busy. One afternoon, rehearsal for their Christmas program was interrupted by men coming from barracks all over the camp. There had been a mail-call. In a prison camp, mail did not wait – it went to the recipient as soon as possible. McCandliss got another letter from his wife.

The earlier letter was not the first his wife had written, but the first one he had received. She assumed he knew. This letter was his present for Christmas of 1944. He learned he was the father of a girl.

*   *   *

Michigan was also cold and snowy. Olive Drew had put up a small tree for Christmas. She had thought about a larger, extravagant one, but knew they would be spending Christmas itself in Muskegon with her mother. The string of lights was out again, but she left it alone. One of her boys could go through the ritual of tracing the twin wires over and around the fragrant green branches. Unscrewing the colored bulb and screwing in a new one from the cardboard pack. Then taking the unscrewed bulb to the next socket and sighing when the chain didn't light up. A yelp of victory when the reds, blues, greens flashed to life. The burned out bulb thrown out immediately lest it get mixed with good ones. They would like that. Make them feel like they were helping her.

They were both coming home. Both her boys. She rated two stars for family on active duty in her window and displayed them proudly. And both fighter pilots; who would have imagined. Young Earl instructing in Texas, Urban a genuine hero, home from England at last. The reporter from the *Detroit Free Press* was coming over, wanted some pictures of her with them both. Their grandmother was almost as proud of them as she was.

She remembered how nice it was to hear Urban's voice when he called from Boston on the twenty-first. He had had to report to someplace called Camp Miles Standish in Rhode Island for a few days. The delay was frustrating, but he would be home Christmas Eve and they would drive across the peninsula to Muskegon.

At first, he thought it was a cold. Headache, runny nose, the sniffles. Heck of a time – ruin Christmas. But the sniffles became sneezes, pain developed in his chest. Ben did not enjoy the meal his mother and grandmother had prepared. He lay down and tried to rest. The next day, they bundled him up, put him in the car, headed for Detroit. The pain grew, he became feverish. The air base at Selfridge was close and it had a military hospital. They took him there. Ben Drew had pneumonia.

Over the next days, he drifted in and out of consciousness.

Flames were bright in his eyes. Red, yellow, intense. Leaping, moving. He was burning. The flames wrapped around his feet, around his legs. They hurt. He smelled himself charring. The canopy was stuck. Fire was everywhere. He couldn't get away. Flames were all around. He had crashed and was hanging upside down in his straps, the weight of the airplane holding him down and yellow-red fire coming after him. He burned. He was in the air, spinning through space. Red-yellow fire came after him. He could not move from the seat. Heat, flames. He was burning.

He woke up with a nurse holding a cool, wet washcloth on his forehead, one hand holding his waving arm down. Ben breathed deeply, looked sheepish. Was I raving again?, he asked. Yes, you were delirious. Was I very loud? Here, have some water. You're doing fine.

Ben thought it odd that his nightmares were about fire. It had not been a conscious worry the whole time he had been flying, even in combat. He had not seen anyone die trapped by fire. He knew of no one in his squadron or the entire group that had burned, yet this was his consistent nightmare while he was hospitalized with pneumonia. He never had such dreams again. The fear of burning in a cockpit must be more of a universal fear among airmen than he realized.

Harold Regan and Jake Wade came to visit. They had been instructors on the *Mustang* with Ben in Florida. The two of them were in the 414th Fighter Squadron flying Republic built P-47s, *Thunderbolts*.

"*Jugs*?" Ben said, "The repulsive thunder box? Damn thing won't get out of it's own way."

"No, no. These are new models. Fast as hell. Bigger wing."

"C'mon, we used those crates to drag targets around at Bartow." The two grinned at him.

"Those were old B models. These are brand new P47N-5s. Boosted, go forever. You'd like them. Come join us."

"No thanks. I figure with my experience, they'll make me an instructor in *Mustang*s again. Or maybe I'll get into our new jet jobs, the P-80s. That would make sense."

She was a good looking girl. She had brown hair cut short with bangs on her forehead. I had no idea who she was or what story she told the hospital to get in. My thoughts were on dates, parked cars, hugs and heavy breathing. I was definitely not prepared for the shock she gave me.

Without a trace of a smile, she walked to the edge of bed and asked, "Are you Lieutenant Drew?" Her look and tone drove out any romantic notions I had. I said I was Ben Drew.

She raised her hand and I prepared for the slap. "You killed my fiancé."

Her hand dropped to her side and she started to sob. "He's dead and you killed him. It's all your fault. He's dead. He's dead."

I had to ask three times before she stopped crying long enough to tell me what was going on. She had been engaged to John Loughead.

Moments passed before I placed the name.

The tears stopped and her look hardened.

Loughead had been the pilot of the Mustang *that had collided with the* B-24 *over Holland.*

Quietly, she said, "You were his flight leader. It was your job to protect him. John's dead. It's your fault. I hate you."

She ran from the room before I could explain the realities of combat flying, the capriciousness of fate. There was nothing, nothing, I could have done. Still, I was shaken.

The 414th was located at Selfridge while they trained with their new airplanes. Regan and Wade came by frequently as long as Ben was hospitalized. They always touted the P-47N. Ben's answer was always the same.

His friends did not visit on New Year's Eve. They had parties to go to. Ben Drew welcomed the New Year of 1945 from a hospital bed – sound asleep.

32

WILMINGTON

Thunderbolt

More train rides were in store for Ben. Long ones. One of the more inefficient policies of the US Army was to send personnel to a Replacement Depot, have them wait, give them their next assignment, then ship them to their new base. Replacement Depots were called "Repo Depots" or "Repple Depples". They were universally disliked. There was little to do and no purposeful work. Junior officers would sometimes shuffle paper and junior enlisted occasionally clean up the base or do KP. It was "make-work." For everyone it was mostly just waiting.

To get to England Ben had gone from Bartow in Central Florida, to the *Repple Depple* in Tallahassee up in the Panhandle, to another depot in New Jersey before getting on a ship. After convalescent and home leave in February, he rode a train from Detroit all the way to the Army Air Force's big replacement center in Santa Ana, California. He hung around waiting for the orders he assumed would take him to a *Mustang* squadron.

He did not get them. He was ordered to Eagle Pass, Texas – the end of the world – to fly AT-6 Texans. Trainers. Not even for advanced tactics – only simple undergraduate flight training. No amount of screaming, hollering or pleading could get the orders changed. He got on another train.

We were stuck in a hole about as far south as you can get and still be in the States. Way down there in the Matamoros, Harlingen area of Texas. I wasn't the only experienced veteran down there either. It didn't take long to figure out that there were just too many of us returning combat pilots and the Army Air Force hadn't a clue what to do with all of us. A lot of talent and savvy was wasted sitting around bases like that. A real backwater. There wasn't even a whole lot of flying. We were usually in the Officers' Club soon after it opened at ten in the morning. A little later for the guys who had to fly with some cadet or on a checkout; which had low priority. I never did any syllabus flights as an instructor. My brother Earl was at nearby Moore Field and we did get to go up in an AT-6 together which was kind of fun.

There was a little town called Piedras Negras across the Rio Grande in Mexico. The Yankee dollar went a long way south of the border. Cheap food, booze and women. We nicknamed the town, "Penis Erect-ass". Learned to drink Tequila. Lots of Tequila. We joked that we sucked so many lemons we'd never get scurvy and that if the Brits were "Limeys", we were "Lemoneys." Real rotgut – it's a wonder we didn't go blind. Or catch something incurable from the senoritas *of the town.*

Between days in the O-club and nights in Piedras Negras, we'd all be confirmed alcoholics in no time at all.. I started to think I'd either have to shoot myself, drink myself to death or get out of the Air Corps. I was desperate. I had to get out of Eagle Pass. So I started looking for strings I could pull. "It's not what you know, it's who you know." I said to myself again and again. I started making phone calls.

Then, one day, I woke up in the morning to find thirty brand new Mustangs parked at the field. They had come in the night before. They were gorgeous. I grabbed my Form-5, my qualification sheet, and my logbook, and went out to Operations. Found the Non-Com in charge of the flight line. "Sergeant, I'd like to sign out one of those Mustangs out there."

"No sir, you can't do that," *he replied.*

"What do you mean I can't do that? I just came back from flying combat in 'em."

"Sir, local regulations say that you have to have 30 hours in the AT-6 before you can check out in the Mustang."

"I've got way more Texan *time than that.*"

"Sorry Sir, it has to be in AT-6's here. CO's orders."

"But I have more time in P-51s than anyone on this base."

"Sorry Sir, that's the rules."

The idiots never did relent. Stupid, power mad little tyrant bucking for higher rank was in charge. That's when I re-doubled my efforts.

At long last I got a call through to my old Group Commander in the 361st, Joe Kruzel. He and I had left England at the same time – we flew our last mission together. He was then the Commanding Officer of Bluenthal Airfield up near Wilmington, North Carolina. I told him I wanted to get back into combat... preferably in England again.

Colonel Kruzel said to me, "Ben, I'd like to go back as much as you would. But since we left the 361st they've had over fifty replacement pilots sent to them. You don't have a ghost of a chance of getting anywhere near the Eighth Air Force again." I was crushed. But he must have had good memories of me, because next he said, "Tell you what. I do have an old buddy from Philippine days, Hank Thorne; that's Colonel Thorne now, who's taking a P-47 group to the Pacific. He's here at Bluenthal and mentioned that he's shy of experienced pilots. I'll ask him."

It worked. Ironically, I was going to the same Thunderbolt squadron Regan and Wade had tried to get me in. I'd have to eat some healthy doses of crow after the bad-mouthing I gave the P-47 when they visited the hospital.

It may sound strange to some that I volunteered to go out and get shot at again, but I couldn't have been happier. I was a warrior, damnit. And there was still a war to be fought.

Ben Drew went to Wilmington, North Carolina to join his new squadron, still a first lieutenant, but now an Ace. He checked in and went to an immediate interview with his new commanding officer, Hank Thorne.

"Drew, when's the last time you flew a Thunderbolt?"

"About two years ago, Sir. We used to pull targets with 'em at Bartow."

Colonel Thorne rose out of his seat. He was over six feet tall. "Don't ever say that around me again."

"Say what, Sir?"

"The 47 is a "rag-dragger" or a target tug. The *Jug* is a damn fine airplane; a real goer."

Ben gulped and said, "Yessir." While thinking, now what have I done? Heck of a beginning in a new outfit.

The Colonel continued, "All of this group's airplanes except mine are in San Francisco getting cocooned for the trip to Iwo Jima on a navy aircraft carrier. Tell you what, you can take her up and get a feel for the N model. You'll like her. More power, longer wings, bigger ailerons, tremendous roll rate; a real sweetheart."

Ben said he'd be pleased to go for a flight.

"And Drew, don't bend her. Not one scratch. You break that airplane and your ass is grass. Understand me?"

"Yessir. Completely Sir."

AAF maintenance logbooks used a "red cross" in a small box next to any system that was inoperative. When Ben reviewed the logs for his new commanding officer's personal airplane that afternoon there were no red crosses. Not a surprise, as it was the CO's airplane.

The P-47N was quite an airplane. A massive improvement over the P-47B he had flown at Bartow. Ben was happy as he cruised north up the coast from Wilmington. He watched the Atlantic surf white-lapping on the beaches of the thin islands called the Outer Banks. Over the engine cowling he could see Cape Lookout hooking into the ocean. He was thinking how great it was to be back flying a modern fighter and humming *I'm Just a Girl Who Can't Say No*.

A pair of dark blue, twin engined airplanes rolled in on him.

The Grumman F7F *Tigercat* was fast, mean and the result of lessons learned over four years of war in the Pacific. A Marine Corps squadron was transitioning to them at MCAS Cherry Point. The two of them would make short work of this errant Air Corps pilot who had wandered onto their turf.

Ben turned into their attack and was surprised to find both Marines behind him after the first turns. The heavy *Thunderbolt* did not turn as well as his *Mustang*. Even with new ailerons. No problem, he thought, I'll go into the gate and use combat boost. That'll show them. He slid the throttle to the outside and pushed it forward into the emergency range – combat power.

The limiting factor on most engines is temperature. A solution is to inject cooling fluid into the cylinders along with the high octane gasoline and supercharged air. For the *Pratt and Whitney* R2800-77 on the latest model P-47N the coolant was Ethylene-Glycol. It was loaded in a special tank and as the throttle came around the gate, the glycol was pumped in with fuel and air to moderate the higher temperature.

The extra power worked. Ben's *Thunderbolt* started to pull away from the scissoring *Tigercats*... until a couple of the piston heads burned through and dense, black smoke poured from the engine.

"Hey Air Corps," came over the radio. "You're on fire."

"Thanks," Ben responded as he headed back to Wilmington, "but I don't need no Marines to tell me."

The smoke was obvious from miles away and the tower at Bluenthal Field asked if Ben was declaring an emergency.

"No. No. No emergency." All Ben could think about was the hell he was going to catch from Colonel Thorne. He wasn't worried about crashing, or burning, he was afraid of what the CO would do.

The tower called out the crash vehicles despite Ben's denials. When the fighter came to a stop, the spitting, smoking engine was sprayed with fog-foam to put out the flames. Ben sat numbly in the cockpit scanning anxiously for what he knew would come. From far across the field a Jeep was approaching at 80 miles an hour.

The Jeep screeched to a halt inches from the airplane and Colonel Thorne leaped out and onto the wing. He ignored the chemical, stinking slop staining his class A uniform and went for Ben's throat. To avoid being strangled, Ben climbed out of the cockpit on the right side. He slipped in the foam on the wing and fell to the ground.

The next morning Ben Drew again found himself at a brace in front of his superior officer's desk. Colonel Thorne had cooled down considerably.

"Lieutenant Drew, yesterday I was ready to court-martial you, if not strangle you first. Well, I've talked to my crew chief and the wing maintenance officer. It seems there should have been a red cross item on my airplane after all."

Ben began to relax a tiny bit. Maybe it wasn't all his fault.

"The combat boost tank had not been filled. There was no Ethylene-Glycol in it."

The Drew grin appeared.

"Stop smiling! I told you not to bend my airplane and you did. It would never have happened if you hadn't gone playing with the Marines. Your hotshot ass is grounded. Five days."

Ben managed a serious "Yessir." There wouldn't be much, if any, flying for the next weeks anyway.

"You need disciplining. No wonder you're still only a first Louie. I know the perfect thing. An officer has to go along with the ground echelon and enlisted troops enroute to Iwo. You will be that officer."

At the time, it seemed a light enough punishment for blowing up the CO's engine. Little did First Lieutenant Ben Drew realize what a stiff sentence it would be.

33

EUROPE

No Fighting

While at Bluenthal, The good news of victory in Europe arrived. Because of Soviet sensitivities, the armistice signed on May 6 was not considered the official one and another was signed in an impressive ceremony on May 8. The fighting in Europe was over. Hitler was dead. There was a new order in Europe; for individuals as well governments. Robert McCandliss was no longer a prisoner. Georg-Peter Eder was.

Bob McCandliss was freed by Tartar troops of the Union of Soviet Socialist Republics. There was no fighting.

Georg-Peter Eder was captured by troops of the United States of America while laying in a hospital bed in Munich. There was no fighting.

Eder's list of claims in the Me 262 had continued to grow. April had started splendidly. He shot down two *Flying Fortresses* and a *Liberator*. His final victory, and combat, was 17 April. South of Berlin, the "Towering Titan", of the 305th Bomb Group, became the last B-17 of the massive 1st Air Division to be shot down. However, Eder was himself shot down by one of the bomber formation's gunners. He suffered a broken left leg and head injuries during his bailout and parachute landing.

By the end, he claimed he had flown 150 missions and shot down twenty-four aircraft in the *Schwalbe*. Only a dozen of these were officially credited to his score. In the late, confused stages of the air war, this was not unusual.

Eder's favorite boast was that not one of the seventeen times he had to bail out or crash in his career was because of an enemy fighter aircraft. He either had a mechanical malfunction, was hit by anti-aircraft fire or downed by the invisible web of bullets thrown out from the bombers he delighted in attacking.

British intelligence wanted to talk to Eder. His American captors transferred him to an POW camp in England.

The first days of freedom for McCandliss had the slow, dreamy unreality of *Alice in Wonderland*. Odd juxtapositions of familiar and strange popped up as he adjusted to his new reality; he was free again, he was not being shot at, he was deep inside Germany, the Nazis had lost.

The liberators of the *Stalag* at Barth were a division of Tartars. Oriental men with high cheek bones and slanted eyes and fearsome reputations frightening to the Germans. For some, suicide was preferable to Tartar vengeance. To the Americans, the Orientals were confusing. They were in Europe, weren't they? The Tartars did not fulfill the German fears. They were well behaved, orderly soldiers. After a few days, they moved on, leaving an authority vacuum in town.

The famous Colonel "Hub" Zemke was the SRO, the Senior Ranking Officer, in the camp. The Germans had vanished overnight. He wielded considerable authority, but months or years of imprisonment had slacked pure military discipline. He was successful in ordering the camp preserved. It would be the *Kriegies* home for some time and, later, be used for refugees. His order to stay in the compound was ignored. The men had been surrounded by barb-wire and guards for too long. They took walks through Barth, through the countryside. Leaves and grass were green with spring. They came back. It was too soon to leave.

The Russians were upset with the Americans. What is the matter with you people? Have you no respect? Your leader has died. Your President Roosevelt is dead and we see no mourning. What is wrong with you?

The ex-POW's made mourning armbands from black tarpaper cut from barracks' roofs. The Russian commissar was happy.

McCandliss and his friends went for walks. On their second day outside, they found a row boat. They would spend hours rowing side by side on the river and bay. The military police had sailboats and could not catch them. In the evening, they hid the boat inside a massive wing, probably from a destroyed glider, in the forest. In the morning, they would drag it into the water and explore some more. The weather was clear and balmy. One afternoon, McCandliss was alone on a small marsh island. He heard quacking and explored further. There was a nest with eggs in the grass and reeds. He carefully placed them in his hat and took them back to his "combine" – the nine men he shared red cross parcels, German rations, materials with. They had their first omelet in more than a year for dinner.

Except for his men wandering about like sightseeing Sunday strollers, Zemke kept good order. When the airlift began, it was the sick and injured who left first. The rest waited for their turn. Prisoners are good at waiting. McCandliss left after eight days.

The American Air Force used B-17s to take the former POW's to France. Each batch of *Kriegies* would be formed into ranks and marched out of the *Stalag*. By the time they were in town, the march became a stroll. The wait at the airfield was pleasant on grass and under newly leafed trees. They were on their way home.

Plywood floors had been fitted across the bomb bays. Canvas straps which passed as seatbelts were tied to the plywood. There were liberal applications of DDT powder and spray to kill all the vermin they probably carried. The B-17 crew was taking no chances. Twelve men sat in the shadowy bomb bay during the take-off and landing. The rest of the time, they crawled all over the airplane, peering out windows and empty gun turrets. The best view was from the nose bubble the bombardier used to use. The pilot of the B-17 gave them a tour. He wanted them to see the damage they had inflicted. He flew all the way across Germany at a thousand feet. The devastation the dozen former prisoners saw was everywhere. Germany had been beaten.

The B-17 landed at Rheims. They walked to Camp "Lucky Strike". On the way, they walked beside a train. One of the cars was filled with brown, wood barrels. The load was wine. The thirsty men tapped into barrels as best they could. Any container served as a cup. Hands worked fine. Some twisted, held their open mouths in the stream and swallowed as fast as they could. They were in fine shape when they reached the repatriation center.

"Lucky Strike" was well named. It had most of the comforts of home. The showers were hot. There was plenty to eat. They were issued new uniforms and underclothes. There were movies. There was one problem—it might take as long as six weeks to leave.

Bob McCandliss wasted no time. He watched. He learned the system so he could beat it. The camp was divided in two. On one side were the men heading home. He watched when roll call was taken. The list was made from men that were there. Name rank and serial number would be shouted out then written down. McCandliss brazened it out. He walked to the outgoing area and fell in with a group that was there.

They were field artillery. Captured as a unit. McCandliss was the only aviator in sight, and one of the few officers. The major in charge of the group looked askance at McCandliss, but did not say anything. His name went on the list with the rest.

Crossing the Atlantic on the SS *Argentina*, the major put the intruding fly-boy in his place. He made McCandliss the supply officer. The ship was crowded. Only designated men could go to the ship's store to buy notions, candy bars and ice cream. For the artillery company that man was McCandliss. Somehow, no matter how carefully he took names and made lists, the money handed him in a flurry always came out short. His early ride home was costing him. He didn't care.

34

PACIFIC

Cows and a Crossing

The first stage of Ben's punishment was a series of long train rides from North Carolina. It should have been a simple trip. The squadron's men were already at Fort Lawton near Seattle – waiting. Ben was traveling alone. However, soon after the train pulled out for the final leg, he was given an unusual challenge.

Since he was still only a first lieutenant, Ben was surprised when the train conductor with his stiff round hat came up to him and told him that he was the senior officer on the train heading for Oregon.

"Me? Are you sure there's no one else?"

"Quite sure. You're the only officer on the train. The other men are all enlisted. I need you to sign this responsibility form."

"Responsibility form? Responsible for what?"

"Oh, just in-charge, you know. Anytime there's troops on board the senior man has to sign. Some army regulation or another." The gray haired conductor tilted his cap back and looked around the car. Most of the soldiers were sleeping or reading. He unfolded the sheet of paper and handed it to Ben.

The letterhead was from some Army Transport Division. The blanks for date, place of departure, train number and destination had already been filled in block letters. Ben glanced quickly over the paragraphs of militarese, took his favorite pen from his pocket, (a *Parker P51*; what was more appropriate than a pen named for the airplane he made his reputation in?) and scrawled "U.L.Drew, 1st Lt., USAAF" on the line at the bottom.

"Thank you very much...", the conductor held the paper at arms length to read the signature, "Lieutenant Drew."

He walked three rows of seats away, then turned as if he had a sudden thought. "By the way, four cars up there are some men who have gotten a hold of some ammunition and are shooting cows. The railroad is already in trouble with farmers in Montana about shooting their cows. Would you please make them stop." He turned abruptly and went on to the next car.

They were drunk. The stink of whiskey breath was there, but an opened window sucked it and the heavy cigarette smoke away. A mean eyed sergeant was staring out the window looking for bovine targets. A M-1 *Garand* was across his knees. Three more rifles leaned against seats and walls. All of them were sergeants. Senior ones. There was six inches of stripes and rockers on every sleeve. Overseas bars lower down. Coats were thrown over seat backs. Above the breast pockets he could see, were combat infantry badges above rows of ribbons. Ties were pulled down or off completely. Shirt sleeves rolled up. They eyed the intruder to see what he would do.

Ben retreated. From their ages he guessed they were pre-war regular army. From their ribbons they were tough, experienced veterans. There was no way they were going to take orders from some twenty year old, first *louie*, flyboy.

On his way back to his seat, Ben thought of a plan. Whenever he traveled he carried two bottles of Jack Daniels finest Tennessee Mash in his bag.

Coming through the door the second time, Ben's tie was gone and the bottle necks were clenched between the fingers of his left hand. He held them up before he said a word.

I was relying on the fact that they had already been drinking and I could stay sober long enough to get the bullets away from them. Well, I wasn't exactly sober by the time I convinced them, but they did give me the ammo. They weren't being deliberately nasty; just tired and bored like we all got on those long, long train rides.

The one guy did squeeze off another shot. Wasn't aiming at anything. Just wanted to clear the chamber before he gave me the clip he said. I must have jumped four feet. They thought that was a riot. Lots of laughs about fraidy-cat fly-boys. Don't remember if I ever told them I had time in combat of my own. We were all unhappy about what we were doing. Not the prospect of more combat. We had whipped the Nazis and were looking forward to knocking out the Nips. It was the train rides, and the long ocean crossings, and the waiting, waiting, waiting we had to do first.

When I left the car they were all passed out cold and I had five clips of 30 caliber ammo in my hand, and the whiskey was all gone. Passing between the cars I threw the clips into the weeds. When I got back to my seat, I put my rolled up coat under my head and took a little nap of my own. I hope the cows of Montana, or wherever we were, were grateful for what I'd done.

Ben was not worried about the voyage across the Pacific; after all, he'd crossed the Atlantic twice. What he hadn't counted on was the slow speed of the *USS Kingsbury* or the vast distances of the Pacific Ocean.

USS Kingsbury was a Liberty Ship. One of the hundreds that came from US shipyards like automobiles came off Detroit assembly lines. They were reliable and carried a great deal of cargo. It may be argued that their numbers were a major factor in winning the war.

Space was at a premium on the ship. The cargo holds were full and the berthing areas crammed with men. Endless chow lines wound through corridors at mealtimes. Navy ships have few places to sit. Deck space was covered with men seeking to get off their feet other than by laying down in their narrow bunks.

Another disadvantage of a slow ship became uncomfortably obvious to all onboard by the second day out. It was hot. A fast ship makes her own wind. Wind that blows down ventilation funnels, into portholes. When there is no surface wind a slow ship generates some breeze, but with even a few knots blowing from astern, the plodding ship's progress cancels the wind and the air is still. Still and hot. The June sun in the Central Pacific is bright and heats what it shines on. There were few electric fans on the *Kingsbury*. The trip from Seattle to Eniwetok in the Marshall Islands lasted two weeks. Eniwetok was the halfway point.

The men dealt with boredom as best they could. Calisthenics were done on deck every morning before the sun's heat became risky. There were meals – and waiting for meals. Movies were shown on the afterdeck when it was dark. There were not many, but it was better than nothing. Talented players, and not so talented men too, had brought musical instruments with them. They organized shows. Ben was something of a singer and performed for the troops a couple of those nights. He performed *Paper Doll*, *That Old Black Magic*, and his favorite, *Oh, What a Beautiful Morning*; he led a sing-along in *Rum and Coca-Cola* and *Mairzy Doats*. There were also boxing "smokers". Ben was pressured to fight as the Air Force representative. He said, "No thanks. I have better sense than to climb into the ring against some big Navy *palooka*." He had all too vivid memories of being forced into the ring with Bill Kemp back in Bottisham. There, he had wound up getting cold-cocked by his friend.

The Eniwetok atoll was a brief stop for fuel and supplies. Only a few navy men went ashore on business while the army hung on the rails and looked longingly at the low, but green, land. They did swap their well worn movies for some new ones. Also well worn.

The next stop was the island of Saipan; five more hot days away. They did get to go ashore there and revel in the relative luxuries of the American bases on the island for a few hours.

Independence Day 1945 was celebrated at sea between Saipan and Iwo Jima with fireworks. The ship's gunners fired tracer rounds from the anti-aircraft cannon, Very pistols shot burning green, white and red flares, and a variety of small arms added their banging for a few, noisy, spectacular moments.

In all, it took twenty-six days for Ben Drew and the men of the 413 Fighter Squadron to cross the Pacific in a cramped Liberty ship. The rest of the pilots, and the squadron's *Thunderbolts*, had crossed in fourteen days in the comfort of a large, and fast, US Navy aircraft carrier. Colonel Thorne's disciplining of Ben Drew was more drastic than either had imagined. But Ben still had not learned.

35

IWO JIMA

Hot Rock

Iwo Jima means "Island of Sulfur". It is a waterless, volcanic ash heap which stinks from sulfur deposits and fumes. Dig thirty feet down and the heat is so high men cannot work more than five minutes.

The volcano Mount Suribachi dominates the south end of island. Airfields were built on the wide flat area across the waist of the island. The Japanese had built two airstrips. The Americans enlarged them and added a third. The Japanese also built sixteen miles of tunnels for defense.

The invasion began on 19 February, 1945. 19,200 United States Marines were wounded. 6,821 were killed. Twenty-seven men earned the Medal of Honor. Admiral Chester Nimitz said that, "On Iwo Jima, uncommon valor was a common virtue."

Iwo sure wasn't much of a place. Once you went to the top of Suribachi, there wasn't much else to do. There weren't even any trees. There were some nurses.

The group officers' club was a converted Quonset hut that we all helped to build. The only three nurses we knew were invited to the opening party. 50,000 men on the island, and the 414th was lucky enough to have women *at our club. However, there was an etiquette problem because of them. My particular job became to construct a separate, outdoor privy for the girls.*

Mustangs *had been flying escort missions from Iwo since April of that year. They were part of the VII fighter command. The group had red diagonal stripped tails on their P-51s. Called themselves the "Sunsetters".*

The day after I got off that slow boat, Colonel Thorne called all his pilots together. We sat on a dune of black volcanic sand while he spoke. Among other things, he said, "There have been many disparaging remarks about this P-47, especially from the Mustang *pilots. Drew, you were a P-51 pilot. I want you and the rest of the boys to take our* Thunderbolts *up and demonstrate them to the people on the air bases on Iwo Jima. I want you to show the* Mustang *pilots what the* Thunderbolt *can do."*

I had to wonder, what exactly did he mean? Demonstrate? How much could we, I, show off? What could we get away with?

While we were building our own club, the squadron would drink with the Mustang *guys. It was easy enough to arrange a "demonstration".*

Once the 413 Squadron's *Thunderbolts* arrived they had to be reassembled and required test flights after the ocean crossing. Ben Drew was assigned P-47N 682, serial number 44-88492. The squadron marked their *Thunderbolts* with an all yellow tail assembly: fins, rudder and elevators. The engine cowling had a wide yellow band and there was a black band around the fuselage. Ben, naturally, called his airplane the "Detroit Miss II", although her name this time was in simple red lettering.

When Ben knew he would be flying one morning, he let it be known to one and all in the club the night before. A pair of *Mustang* pilots took him up on the dare and arranged to be in the air when Ben took off.

The *Mustangs* dropped behind Ben's tail. He did a series of ever tighter turns getting a feel for his new mount. It was a good airplane, but no match for a P-51. However, he knew from his combat over

Europe that a pilot's skill and daring could cancel differences in airplanes. He pulled out all the stops. He ran the *Mustang* pilots ragged, but they had started with the advantage and he could not shake them. The flight's maneuvering took them over the slopes of the island's dominating, single, volcanic mountain —Suribachi.

The marines maintained a defensive camp at the top of Mount Suribachi. Even at this late date, Japanese soldiers remained on the island hidden deep in defensive caves. Their code of *Bushido* would grant honor and eternal glory to any man who could tear down the hated American flag at the top of the island. There had been a series of suicidal Jap attacks so the American Marines were more than a little trigger happy. Granted, the last two weeks had been quiet, but there was no way of telling when another attack would come.

There was always the noise of airplanes flying from the airfields and the marines on the mountain were fairly used to it, but this time the sound was growing louder fast. The marines stood on top of their sand-bagged trench, looked down the steep slope and saw a giant round engine and huge, shimmery prop disk coming straight at their heads. This stupid bastard was trying to kill them! They hit the dirt. At the bottom of their trench, they rolled over and looked up. In the instant the big airplane was overhead, they noticed silver wings, the black anti-glare panel, the egg shaped bulge of canopy and the head and legs of the pilot. The stupid bastard was flying upside down. Two more airplanes followed – higher – and right side up.

It was not what Colonel Thorne had in mind. Drew was grounded again. There were too many complaints to ignore. He sat for six days while the group flew their first missions – long ones. It was 750 nautical miles from Iwo Jima to Honshu. The group's mission was destruction of ground targets.

Ben was on duty in the control tower on top of the Operations Building during a strange occurrence. Each of the squadrons provided an officer for liaison with the airfield. Since he was grounded, Ben had this duty assigned to him. There was a communications center as part of the operations building. When things were quiet, as they were that day, the officers would spell each other. Ben was the only officer around. At the time, it was just another day, but the date would become famous.

In the morning he looked up and saw three B-29s circling overhead at about 10,000 feet. There was nothing unusual about B-29s over Iwo Jima; it was their emergency landing field and a navigation fix between Japan and their bases in the Marianna Islands. However, the bombers were usually in large formations and rarely circled. Ben asked the sergeant who worked in the control center why there were only three. He got a classic army shrug in return. "I don't know, Sir. No idea at all."

Late that afternoon, a single *Superfortress* flew over Iwo Jima heading south. This time Ben was near the radio and heard the call to "Hot Rock" which was the callsign for the Iwo Jima control center. "Hot Rock, Hot Rock. Pass to Tinian, mission accomplished."

The sergeant used the teletype to pass the message as requested. Neither of them had any idea what it was about.

The next day, the world learned that an "atomic weapon of massive destructive force" had been dropped on Japan. Neither Ben Drew nor any of the men on Iwo Jima had heard of anything like an atomic bomb before and it did not mean much then. They continued to fly missions.

Ben later flew over Nagasaki. He had seen the cities of Germany that the RAF and USAAF had bombed. They were nothing by comparison. The destruction of Nagasaki was complete. Nothing in the city was left standing.

Harold Regan was my wingman. The same guy who had been instructing with me in Bartow. Same one who visited me in the Detroit hospital. He had endured all those months instructing and finally got his chance to go to war. This was his first time out and he was really eager. I remember telling him lessons learned the hard way. "When we do strafing, spread out, my friend, don't tuck in behind your flight leader. 'Cause if you do, everything they're throwing up at the leader is going to come into you. So make two targets, not one big one." He didn't listen… or he forgot.

The flight up to Japan was monotony made solid. Worse than it ever was in Europe. The Jap air force was pretty well beaten back to the home islands, so there was no need for a good look-out doctrine and the tickle of adrenaline that bogies might be called any second was missing. Plus, there was nothing to look at. Nothing. Underneath was blue Pacific or white cloud for hours on end. We didn't even have bombers to watch or screw around with. The squadron was alone. The job of the 414th was not to escort bombers. As I understood it, after the invasion of Japan, we would move to the first airfield captured and fly close air support for the troops on the ground. This mission was almost an area check out. No bombs, no rockets. Couldn't lug them the distance. The eight fifties on our Thunderbolts were loaded 'though.

Like at Achmer, I was always scanning the ground as well as the sky. Sure enough, near Nagoya, down on Akenagohara airfield there was bunch of Mitsubishi bombers; the ones we called "Betty". I peeled off and went after them. Regan stayed with me.

Akenagohara was heavily defended. As the pair of *Thunderbolts* came over, the *Flak* opened up. Ben could see streams of tracer passing beneath his airplane. Regan had stayed too close to his leader. Anti-aircraft fire aimed at Ben hit him instead.

"I'm hit. I'm hit."

Ben turned to the coast and swung out to watch Regan. "Can you climb, four?"

"Yeah, doing OK. Shaking pretty bad 'though."

"C'mon, buddy, see if we can nurse that airplane to the beach. Get off shore."

Off the coast were submarines and airplanes waiting to rescue downed airmen… if they could nurse their damaged airplanes far enough. They had to fly one hundred, one hundred fifty miles to get away from patrolling Japanese vessels. Special B-29s carried rafts they could drop, extra equipment, and high powered radios. Navy submarines or flying boats would make the pickup, take the men to safety.

Regan's P-47 struggled up to 11,000 feet before the engine began to lose power. He started slowly down, exchanging altitude for distance from the Japanese coast. He nursed his airplane 220 miles before the *Pratt and Whitney* began to smoke and lose more power. Regan called Ben, "Don't think I can keep her in the air much longer." He was holding the nose up trying to stretch the glide. Trying to stay in the air.

"Keep your speed up, buddy. It's time to get out. Roll the canopy back. Get over the side before you spin."

Regan waited too long. Held the *Thunderbolt's* nose up too long. He panicked. The opened canopy and his standing body dragged the heavy airplane into a spin. As he cleared the cockpit, he was thrown back into the horizontal stabilizer.

Ben flew circles around the descending parachute. He followed it down to the wave tops. Regan had his life jacket and raft inflated, but for some reason, had not crawled into the raft. He waved his arm. Ben climbed to establish contact with the rescue aircraft.

The B-29 got a radio bearing and came closer. The crew asked Ben to continue orbiting overhead until they got there. A submarine must have been in the area because it surfaced at the same time the B-29 arrived. Endurance for fighters over Honshu was less than twenty minutes before they had to head back. Ben had been out much longer than that.

The B-29 flew low and dropped a large raft. Ben watched Regan swim over and put an arm through one of the loops hanging from the side. Ben could do no more. He flew low over his friend and dipped a wing. He got a weak wave in reply.

Alone, Ben climbed back to altitude and took up a heading he hoped would take him to Iwo Jima. His radios were almost burned out by all the transmitting he had been doing. He also was not positive where he was because of all his low altitude maneuvering over Regan. He was using dead reckoning of the most desperate sort – by guess and by God. A heading error more than five degrees would make him miss Iwo's four and a half mile width.

Hours went by. Ben had everything pulled back. The prop was turning so slowly he swore he could count the blades. He tried every trick to save what little fuel he had left.

"*Hot Rock, Hot Rock,* this is *Nevada Blue Three.* Over." From what he thought was one hundred miles out he started calling on Iwo's emergency frequency. "*Hot Rock, Hot Rock,* this is *Nevada Blue Three.* Over."

Out of desperation, Ben turned his radio off to see if letting it cool down would help. Lights came on for fuel low warning. He turned the radio back on. "*Hot Rock, Hot Rock,* this is *Nevada Blue Three.* Over."

Silence.

Ben rolled the canopy back, removed his shoulder straps. The slipstream swirled around him as he pressed the transmit button one last time.

"*Hot Rock, Hot Rock,* this is *Nevada Blue Three.* Over."

Very faintly through his earphones, Ben heard, "Aircraft calling *Hot Rock,* say again."

"*Hot Rock,* this is *Nevada Blue Three.* Request DF steer. One, two three, four, four, three, two, one." The short count was enough, they gave him a steer to Iwo Jima.

The steer was 100 degrees magnetic.

Ben had flown well past the island. If he had gone down, the rescuers would never have looked in that direction.

The tip of Mount Suribachi had never looked so good. The radio was weak and on its last legs as Ben called for a straight-in approach to the center strip.

As the P-47 touched down the engine burped and quit. The big four bladed propeller had stopped turning long before Ben braked the airplane to a stop.

The submarine that picked up Regan brought him straight to Iwo Jima where he was transferred to the base hospital. The next day, the 413 CO, Major Paul Wignall, told an obviously concerned Ben Drew, "Just talked to the hospital. Regan's going to be all right. He's seating up in bed and talking. Both of his legs are covered with plaster, but he's OK. Maybe tomorrow you and some of the boys can go over and see him."

There was no tomorrow. That night, Ben's wingman, Harold Regan from Spokane, Washington, suffered a massive brain hemorrhage and died. The collision with the tail of his spinning *Thunderbolt* had broken both his legs. Those injuries the doctors found. What had gone unnoticed was a fractured skull.

The Akenagohara mission was flown on the day the Japanese surrendered. The Second World War was over.

36

SAIPAN

Bureaucracy Bungles

The war was over.
 No one was shooting anymore.
 No one was getting killed.
 Life on Iwo Jima was worse than ever.
 The island still stank of sulfur. Nothing green was growing yet. Land mines went off at odd times. There was no flying. It was time to go home.
 But they could not.
 Rotation home was based on a complex "points" system. Points were assigned for missions flown, medals awarded, months served overseas, whatever else the powers that be deemed appropriate. Ben and his tent-mates figured they would be naturals for the first to leave. When they asked, they were told, "There are 375,000 men on this island. You'll go when they are ready to go. Wait your turn."

We were stewing. It wasn't fair. The tent I was in was all vets. We should have been on our way home. Bobby McDowell had flown P-47s in the Western Desert and did another tour in the CBI. Then there was Doc Moers. Doc wasn't a nickname; he was the squadron flight surgeon. Had left a very comfortable private practice to do his bit. He was the oldest of our group. I was the youngest. Doc had a biting wit when he spoke which wasn't often. The real character of the group was "Mooch-head" Murdoch. "Mooch" was the most unlikely Lieutenant-Colonel in the entire air force. He had been the group's operations officer. Never seemed to get his clothes washed.

While we were hanging around on Iwo, the group commander thought he had figured a way to get at Murdoch for his sloppy habits. Colonel Thorne ordered him to take the entire group inspection; that's 700 men. Since his trousers were filthy and there wasn't time to get them laundered, Mooch cut the legs off with a knife and took the review wearing "shorts".

He had quite a life. Before the war, he had been called the greatest jockey in the state of Virginia. A couple of years after, he was a Senior Vice President of the First National City Bank of New York. I suppose he paid somebody to clean his pants.

The rumor circulating on Iwo was that control of going home was on Saipan in the Mariannas... if you could get there.

They waited, played interminable card games, lost all their money, won the money back, walked, talked and drank what strictly rationed alcohol was available. One day a B-29 *Superfortress* landed at the airfield. The quartet rushed up to the plane commander. "Where you headed? Saipan. Great. Can you take us with you?"

The plane commander was more than cooperative. "Orders? Nah, ya don't need 'em. Just get on. Glad to take you"

"Can you give us thirty minutes?"

"Sure. It'll take that long to gas this baby."

Ben and his buddies screamed off to their tent in Mooch's jeep. They threw their footlockers and bags in the back of the Jeep, piled in on top or hung from the sides and sped back to the airstrip. As they got out of the Jeep, Mooch exultantly threw the keys high into the air and yelled, "Goodbye, Iwo Jima!"

Saipan was the operational center for army forces in the theater. That part of the rumor was correct. Our heroes headed for Headquarters Building and their ride home. They handed their orders to the camp commandant's sergeant clerk who took them into an inner office. Moments later they were confronted by a US Army full colonel –riding boots and breeches, silver eagles gleaming on starched collar, tie carefully and tightly knotted, brown leather riding crop tucked under one arm. "Gentlemen. You Air Corps types got all the breaks. You got all the press. You lived soft. And in my book you didn't deserve one damned bit of it. You are going to sit in this camp until all, and I mean all, of my army troops go home. If it takes two years, it will be fine with me." He held up their orders and slowly ripped them in half. He let them drop and as they fluttered to the floor, gave the four pilots a tight-lipped smile. "Now get out of here."

Life on Saipan was hell.
Hell lasted three months. Murdock had been at Harvard with one of the Boston Kennedy sons. The situation was harsh enough that it was time to pull strings, to bring influence to bear. It worked.
In November of 1945, the irrepressible quartet were summoned to Colonel Riding Crop's office. The colonel was not in a good mood. He held up a sheaf of papers like they were used toilet paper. "Wise guys, huh. OK, you want to be on a ship out of here. Well, I'm giving you your wish. I found the slowest goddamn boat in the US Navy; just for my favorite flyboys – a Liberty ship – a real barge. Should take about a month to get across the Pacific." His grin was sadistic as he passed their orders to his sergeant clerk. "Enjoy the trip. Dismissed."
Colonel Riding-Crop's estimate was not far off. The trip from Saipan to Portland, Oregon took twenty-seven days. On the fourth day, there was no fresh water for showers. The Air Force officers bathed in salt water with soap developed for the purpose. It left a gritty, slimy feel on the skin. Fresh vegetables had gone the day before. Even cabbages for

the mess cooks' trick of making salad of that long lasting vegetable were gone by the ninth day. All the "passengers" had to eat was powdered eggs and canned meat. Spam. And potatoes, lots of potatoes. And rice. And bread. Coffee, thick and black, navy style, was their only luxury. Other than coffee and water, they drank "Bug Juice". Bug Juice began as concentrated fruit flavoring and sugar reduced to powder and kept in palm size packets. It would keep forever. Sometimes it would turn as solid as rock, but that made no difference as the first step in preparation was to dissolve the packet's contents in a pint of water. If the lump was solid it simply took longer to dissolve. The resulting liquid would take the chrome off car bumpers and dissolve paint. It was cut with four more gallons of water before being served... usually at room temperature.

The crew of the ship ate normally and well, in their own mess. Their mess was off limits to all 400 troops on board; including the officers. The cooking aromas of chicken and beef spread throughout the ship and made their culinary penance all the worse.

Any form of drinking alcohol is absolutely, totally, and unforgivingly forbidden aboard a United States Navy ship. The usually hard drinking pilots found themselves suddenly and unhappily on the wagon.

A Christmas Celebration—1945
(L-R) Bill McCoppin, Marie Kemp (sister), Ben Drew, Bill Kemp, Betty Lee Kemp (wife)

36

MICHIGAN

A.N.G.

The returning pilots jumped, rather than fell, off the wagon. When they stepped on dry land in Portland, Oregon, their first order of business was to rent a hotel suite and have one whale of a party for forty-eight hours. Memory of the time was fuzzy, but included "lots of booze, lots of women, and lots of hangovers."

A big personnel transfer center to handle the waves of returning servicemen was in Portland. Most of his hangover remained the morning Ben went to the center for out-processing. It was a walloping hangover, the kind the Germans call a *katzenjammer*, so Ben was not pleased when the first clerk he had to deal with, asked why he wasn't wearing his Captain's bars. Ben could not believe the question. He made the clerk go through his record. It turned out his promotion papers had been chasing after him for over seven months. The hangover was forgotten. The back pay alone made the new rank a good deal. He signed his name in a dozen places on originals and carbon-copies. When the clerk handed him the now fat envelope with all his records, Ben asked him for a set of captain bars. The corporal said, "Oh, we don't give out the insignia. Just stop by any Army-Navy store for a set. There's one down the street.

That's how I wound up pinning on my own captain's bars in a grubby, little store in Portland. It was almost as bad as getting my Distinguished Flying Cross thrown over the wall of a privy. Not that it made any difference. I was really proud of that promotion. Relieved too. Second to first lieutenant is no big deal; practically automatic. Making captain meant that that 104th article of war was finally out of my record.

I bought enough bars to go on my shoulders and collars so I could wear my new rank on the long train trip to Chicago.

Once again, Ben was informed that he was the senior officer on the train. As the conductor handed him the Responsibility Form, Ben asked, "Have you been having any problems with cows on this line?" When the conductor looked confused, Ben laughed as he remembered the GI's with rifles. "Never mind. Private joke from the last time I 'bought' the train."

"Yessir," said the conductor looking at the signed form, "Captain Drew, we do have a bunch of soldiers who are being awfully rowdy a couple of cars back. The Polish-American club back in Portland helped 'em celebrate the end of the war and they kind of overdid it."

Ben first went straight to his own bag and got out the two bottles of Jack Daniels before he went back to the car with the soldiers. By the time the whiskey was gone, he was the best of buddies with the men, most of whose names he could not pronounce and ended in "ski".

Urban L. "Ben" Drew, 812776, was discharged from the United States Army Air Force in Chicago. He went home to Detroit.

One afternoon the telephone rang and Mrs. Drew answered it. Holding her hand over the mouthpiece, she called, "Ben, the governor is on the phone."

"Sure, Mom, sure he is. What governor?" His mother was not prone to practical jokes; why would the governor call him?

"The governor of Michigan, Governor Kelly. And he wants to speak with you."

Ben heard the governor say, "Captain Drew, I am starting up the Michigan Air National Guard again and I want you to participate."

Ben's first response was that he did not know anything about the National Guard.

Governor Kelly told him that was all right as there were a lot of sergeants left over from the pre-war 107th Observation Squadron and they would know what to do. He had been specifically recommended for the job along with Captain Steffy and Colonel Armstrong.

Colonel Armstrong would be the commanding officer of what would become the 127th Group. He had flown B-24s in the Eighth Air Force over Europe. Ben would become a major and be his Director of Operations. Captain Steffy had flown fighters in the Pacific, earned a DSC and would be Assistant Operations.

It was a dream assignment for men who loved to fly. They were combat officers. They knew how to operate. They could learn the administration, organization and politics that went with the peacetime military.

Ben coordinated rudder and aileron as the nose come back to the horizon. The airplane had gone up, over and around in an almost perfect barrel-roll. Ben grinned at the pleasure of the maneuver. He looked over at the crew chief in the right seat. The sergeant's eyes were as wide as a surprised owls. His mouth opened and closed twice, before he gulped and said, "Damn. Damn, that's the first time I've ever been upside-down in an *Invader*. Damn. Didn't even know a bomber could roll like that. Damn."

Ben laughed. "Well, hang on. I'm going to try a loop next." He checked that both R-2800 engines were at full power as he pulled straight back on the yoke. The Douglas built medium bomber looped just fine.

The Michigan Air National Guard was formed with two squadrons of *Mustangs* and one squadron of B-26 *Invaders*. As part of the headquarters staff Ben got to fly both types. His checkout in the Invader was minimal. Most checkouts in those days were. "Show me how to start it and I can fly anything," was the prevailing attitude. Part of Ben's job as operations was to provide serious justification for their flight hours and budget. It was difficult when the reality was closer to a flying club than a military unit. The experience level of the "citizen-soldier" pilots and mechanics was high. There were no new-boys to break in. Best of all, nobody was shooting at them. "Training" justified all sorts of fun flying. Debriefs were held in the bar where the rules were, "The first liar doesn't stand a chance" and "He who yells loudest wins."

In 1948 after the Air Force became an independent service, Michigan's newly elected Governor Sigler choose Major Ben Drew to be Michigan's first Air Adjutant General, a position normally filled by a brigadier general. The post was a high level and important one. In addition to his duties in Michigan, Ben spent a lot of time working at the Pentagon. He enjoyed the work and started to think about making the Air National Guard a career.

However, the senior army officers of the national guard had not taken well to what they thought of as "that upstart, overrated new service". The general in command was especially possessive of what he considered "his" budget and was certainly not about to give up a dollar more than he had to.

The situation came to a head when the squadrons went to Grayling, Michigan for the summer encampment and exercises.

Ben had been struggling to get the Air Guard its fair share of the budget and as a result was constantly at odds with the general. As Ben described Grayling, "There were holes in the runway so big, you could lose a *Mustang* in one. And there was the damn army building a brand new officers' club. I'd had it."

Ben called Bobby Ball who was the aviation editor for the *Detroit News*. They had always gotten along well and like most reporters, he was usually looking for a story. The next day Ball's article lambasting the National Guard, the commanding general and, by implication, the governor, was on the front page. Going to the press was not one of the more politic things Ben had ever done.

The day after the article appeared, Governor Sigler telephoned Ben. "Drew, I want your resignation on my desk in twenty-four hours."

So ended the military career of Urban L. Drew.

37

AFRICA

One War Was Over

Ben became a college student again. He had seen the advantage of formal education and like many of his contemporaries took advantage of the GI Bill to go to school. His roommates at the University of Michigan were Bill McCoppin, who had followed Ben down during the attack at Achmer; his brother Earl, who soon left for the University of California; and "Gimper" Grant, who had been a navigator on B-17s and a POW. Ben took only two years to earn his Bachelors degree.

Ben's first civilian job was with the Fram Corporation in Denver. He was in marketing and distribution and kept his hand in aviation by flying the corporation's *Beech-18*. He moved to Washington State in 1953 as Vice-President of Columbia Air Service. Soon after, he married Mary Elizabeth Breitenstern from one of Denver's oldest families. They had a son David in 1955. Beginning in 1956, he flew with Slick Airways as a captain on domestic and international routes in C-46, DC-4 and DC-6 equipment. When Slick foundered, Ben and nine other ex-Slick captains formed American International Airways. He became the Vice-President for Operations. He remained with AIA for a year before starting his own airline in Europe.

Headquarters for Seven Seas Airlines was in Amsterdam. The airline flew charters to all parts of Europe, Africa and the Americas. Seven Seas began as a typical non-scheduled airline; anywhere, anytime, for a buck. Gradually, the airline began to make money. More and more of their flights went into the Belgian Congo. The airline expanded. They had more airplanes, more pilots.

There was a civil war going on in the Congo and Ben was in the thick of it. He was a personal acquaintance of Moise Tshombe; they would drink beer together. Seven Seas set up an office in Elisabethville in the secessionist Katanga Province. Business was good until United States policy changed and contracts with the United Nations were canceled. The airline went broke. Ben lost a fortune

Ben Drew started another airline, this time working out of the Ton Son Nhut airport in South Viet Nam. This lead to a business exporting monkeys to the United States, England and France to manufacture drug serums. The increasing war in South East Asia and the development of laboratory developed serums ended this successful business.

The full story of Ben Drew in the Congo and Viet Nam would make a book by itself. Perhaps, it will be written… someday.

Calair International developed installations of Westinghouse J-34 jet engines for increased performance on several types of transport aircraft. Ben became Calair's sales manager and was involved with their engineering program. He flew prototype aircraft on test and demonstration flights. He spent a lot of time in Alaska.

Ben Drew became an independent aircraft broker in 1968. He arranged sales and leases on Douglas DC-8, Boeing 707 and Lockheed *Electra* airplanes worldwide from his base in West London, UK.

In 1973, while on business in Hong Kong, he met Lynette Cronje. The pert, dark haired *Afrikaner* swept him off his feet. She was from an old South African family and worked with the Foreign Minister. They married soon after they met and divided their time between a flat in London and the house they bought in Pretoria, Lynette's hometown.

** The other *Katzenjammer Kid*, Bill Kemp, moved to Arizona. When the war ended, he became one of the initial cadre who founded the Arizona Air National Guard. For a time, he was Barry Goldwater's pilot. Eventually, he resigned from the ANG and returned to the telephone line work he had done before joining the Army Air Force. He was killed in a car crash in 1966.

** Robert McCandliss had orders to Florida for training to return to a fighter group. He was riding a train with Virginia and their baby, when, at a stop along the way, he read of Japan's surrender. His request for release was granted almost immediately.

He went back to MIT, completed a degree in Mechanical Engineering and, later, a Masters in Nautical Architecture. He was hired by Electric Boat in Groton, Connecticut. There, he was on the design team of the US Navy's first nuclear powered submarines; *Nautilus* and *Seawolf*. He remained at Electric Boat through the beginnings of the Nuclear Attack and Fleet Ballistic Submarine programs, then went to Litton Corporation to design a new class of navy frigate. The frigates were built in Pascagoula, Mississippi and he moved there to set up the program.

The daughter he waited so long to see, gave him two grandchildren and five great grandchildren.

**Leonard Wood finished his tour with 74 missions and instructed stateside until the end of the war. He received a degree in Geology from Michigan State and went to work for the US Geological Service. He had joined the Michigan ANG in 1949 and was recalled during Korea for 21 months with the Air Defense Command. After release from active duty the USGS assigned him to Texas (where he flew with the Texas ANG), Colorado and headquarters in Washington, DC. He has retired and lives in Oakton, Virginia.

** Bill McCoppin first worked for the Pennsylvania Rail Road and later became an airline pilot. When he retired, he was flying 300 passenger DC-10s as a senior American Airlines pilot. A long way from a P-51 fighter.

** William Rogers, Ben's frequent wingman and with him during the attack on the Blohm and Voss flying boat, became a dentist in Michigan. He constructed a house of logs in Wisconsin for his retirement.

** *Red* Rowlett, deputy leader at Achmer and one of the pilots in the Bottisham Four photograph, made the Air Force a career and retired in Hutchinson, Kansas.

** The pilot of *Suzy G*, Frank Glankler, became a cotton broker in Memphis, Tennessee. His wife and airplane's namesake passed away in 1998. Frank followed her a year later.

** Joe Kruzel remained in the service and became a two star general in the USAF.

** In 1948, Colonel Christian's widow remarried and her new husband formally adopted her daughter Lou Ellen. Lou married and had a daughter, Heather Christian Fleming, and son, Reid Blair Fleming, of her own. Her name is now Lou Christian Loving and she resides in Austin, Texas.

38

PRETORIA

Award

In 1974, a producer at the British Broadcasting Company called Ben. The BBC was about to do a documentary on the Luftwaffe's "Washington Bomber", would Mr. Drew be willing to participate? Ben said he would be more than happy to assist, but why were they asking him?

"Heavens, man, didn't your own people tell you? In 1944, you sank the world's largest aeroplane at Lake Schaal."

For thirty years, Ben had accepted that the flying-boat his flight had shot-up was a *Blohm and Voss BV222*. That is what the official combat report said. The misgivings he, Travis and Rogers had about calling it a *BV222* came back to him. They were right; the monster had not been a *Viking*, but something bigger. At the time of their debrief, no one had heard of the *BV238*.

Late in 1940, the Blohm and Voss works began work on a flying-boat large enough to carry out Hitler's plan of bombing Washington and New York. Post-war inspection of German records showed the first prototype conducted flight tests on Lake Schaal until it was destroyed by strafing *Mustang*s. The sinking set *BV238* development back many months. Three other *BV238*s were under construction; none of them ever flew.

When the BBC learned this, they sent divers into the lake. The divers reported there was nothing left but the Daimler-Benz engines. After the producer learned that Ben Drew had a London address, he was a natural for the show. A limousine took Ben to the studios for preliminary conferences. A request was made to the US Archives to locate the gun-camera films. There was no doubt about it, all the facts matched ; First Lieutenant U.L.Drew leading A flight of the 375th Fighter Squadron had destroyed the "Washington Bomber", the *BV238*.

Ben made sinking the world's largest airplane a point of pride. When the war stories started, destruction of the *BV238* was only a notch below his double *Me262* kill. He had every reason to brag a little – it was a unique event.

Although he kept his London flat, Ben moved his primary residence to Pretoria, South Africa. From there, he continued to broker sales and leases of jet transports. He cut some profitable deals with South African Airways' old airplanes. He also tried a new venture; for several years, he divided his time between Pretoria, London and the wilds of the Caprivi Strip in what was then South West Africa, today's Namibia, while setting up Caprivi Air Lines. He called Caprivi Air the "Situtunga Line" after the large antelope found in the lush swamps of the Okavango. The airline's logo featured the graceful horned head of a *Situtunga*. The airline did not succeed. There was a war going on in that part of the world and, in addition to restrictions to where and when he could fly, the South African Air Force was transporting his potential passengers for free.

Late one evening in '83, the phone rang and the voice on the other end asked, "Is this Major Urban Drew?"

Major? I figured it had to be some of my friends at a local pub pulling a fast one. I made what I thought was an appropriately rude comment. When the voice identified itself as General so-and-so, I really got sarcastic.

Exasperated, the poor guy said, "I beg your pardon, but I am very serious. I will read you what I was given. 'A grateful nation, albeit some forty years late, is to award you the highest decoration the United States Air Force can give for extraordinary heroism in aerial combat against an armed enemy of the United States.' It is signed by General Charles Gabriel, Chief of Staff of the United States Air Force."

I didn't know what to say. That call was the first I learned of getting a medal for something I had done thirty-nine years earlier.

In 1983, Urban L. Drew was awarded the Air Force Cross. The United States Air Force had begun reviewing old award recommendations. Major Vivienne Veach, a Public Relations Officer, had found the paperwork which had recommended a Distinguished Service Cross be awarded to Drew for his shootdown of the two *Messerschmitt 262s*. For some obscure reason the DSC had never been approved; never been awarded. Her job was to correct such oversights. She felt that Ben Drew deserved the nation's second highest award for valor. The chain of command agreed with her. As did a special congressional review committee. Of course, the Air Force could no longer award the DSC. It was an Army award. The equivalent medal since the Air Force became an independent service was the Air Force Cross.

Despite the embargo of South Africa, the United States Air Force had a regularly scheduled logistics flight to Johannesburg. A vital NASA and Air Force space tracking station was in the country. The USAF arranged for Ben and Mrs. Drew to ride the C-141 *Starlifter* to Washington.

The ceremony took place in the Pentagon offices of the Secretary of the Air Force. Olive Drew came up from Florida and Ben's son, David, was there to make it a family reunion. Models of an F-16 and B-1 bomber on the secretary's coffee table were reminders of progress made since the event being honored.

Secretary Vern Orr was a tall man. Before he leaned over to pin the light blue ribbon and bronze medal on Ben's chest, he said, "I have been the president's air force secretary for seven years and never had the occasion to pin an Air Force Cross on anyone. I am sure you are honored, but it is just as much an honor for me."

Ben returned to Pretoria a proud and happy man.

Secretary of the Air Force Vern Orr pinning the Air Force Cross on Urban Drew

39

WIESBADEN

Hospital

The bells rang on the quarter hour. A traditional pattern. Ding-dong at fifteen past the hour. Twice that at half-past. Six crisp rings at forty-five minutes. And on the hour, four ding-dong pairs, eight echoing rings, followed by slow paced bongs in a different key. One for each hour gone in the two halves which make a day. The bells never stopped. In the afternoon, when the windows were open, two sets could be heard. One soft and distant, one close and loud. Ben never learned whether the bell towers were in a church or some ancient *burghall*.

The bells echoed backwards. Bells are not electronic timers accurate to frivolous seconds. Their clockwork mechanisms have kept time for generations and they may be forgiven their own pace. The distant clock chimes rang first. Except on the hour, their soft peals ended as the near and loud began. A long echo in reverse. The distant echo the apparent cause of the close-by ringing of the bells. Their strange pairing not only marked the passage of time, but questioned the perception of memory. Is the past a fact, or is it the result of human feelings and emotion, perception and imagination, hate and love?

The bed dominated the room. Shiny metal cleverly arranged to go up, down, tilt, lean and stretch. Posts, hinges and rods were all stainless silver. Underneath, actuator rods shining from two inch diameter tubes.

Their white paint yellowed at the seams where oily lubricant oozed out. The rods bright and slick where they twisted the bed up and down, slanted and straight. The bed made its passenger look small.

A tangle of wires and tubes climbed like vines from holes and sockets in the wall. Some reached up the shiny metal limb arcing above. A button much like a bomb release, at the tip of a thin plastic tendril, was pinned to the pillow.

In the bed, Georg-Peter Eder was dying.

The fighter pilots' world is a small one. During a war they are intent on killing one another, but as the years of peace go by, they find they have more in common with each other than the causes they once fought for. Meetings become common. Former enemies share tables at symposia, book and picture signings. They embellish each other's stories; repeating them until the performance is smooth and entertaining. Americans, Germans, English all have their fighter pilots' organizations, newsletters, reunions. So do the other nations that fought in World War Two.

When the USAF released the story of Drew's Air Force Cross along with the story of 7 October at Achmer, Eder got in touch with Ben through the *Gemeinschaft der JagdFlieger E.V.* and the American Fighter Aces Association. Eder had been at Achmer that day. From where he stood he had a ringside seat to the combat and added details and corroboration.

They began to correspond regularly and Ben visited Eder and his wife, Martha, in Wiesbaden. With interpreter help from Mrs. Drew and historian Hans Rossbach, they got along famously. Ben had his recent Air Force Cross with him. Not to be outdone, Eder pulled out his Knight's Cross with Oak Leaves. *Touché.*

Naturally, the Eders were invited to come to South Africa.

After the war, Eder had a moderately successful career as a cattle auctioneer. He was not wealthy, but could afford a couple of tourist class tickets to Johannesburg. He called Pretoria and announced that he would be arriving in two days.

Ben had connections throughout the aviation world of southern Africa. Military and civil. He called in some favors. He told the director of South African Airways about his guest coming from Germany. When the Eders checked in for their flight, they were surprised to learn they would be traveling first class. Not only first class, but with special VIP treatment on orders from the director of SAA himself.

The captain of the Boeing 747 had been told that he had a special passenger on board and put the former fighter pilot in the co-pilot's seat for part of the flight. In the course of conversation he had asked Eder, "Who the hell do you know at SAA?"

Eder's English was not very good. He had been studying just to talk to Ben, but had a ways to go. Fortunately, Lynn Drew spoke not only Afrikaans and English, but French and German. She translated for the two warriors when the conversation became too complex for Ben's poor German and Eder's poorer English.

Late one evening, after wine with dinner and with a KWV Brandy in his hand, Eder quietly expressed his motivation during the war. No translation was needed for *"Ein Reich, Ein Volk, Ein Führer"*

The South African Military Museum at the Saxonwald has one of the few remaining two seat *Me262s* in existence. Naturally, a visit was arranged. The curator himself took the two old fighter pilots on a tour. Barricades, ropes, Do-not-touch signs meant nothing. He was honored to have such guests. He saved the *262* for last. The long canopy had been carefully opened. Steps moved alongside. Cushions placed in the seat buckets to make up for the parachutes that pilots would normally have sat on. A work stand had been moved close to give the photographer better angles. The result was a remarkable photograph.

Georg-Peter Eder sat in the front seat the entire time. After he first climbed in, Ben, the curator, and the small crowd had been silent, watching as Eder ran his hands over controls he remembered from more than thirty years before. The twin throttles on the left, large fuel levers sticking out next to them. Under his right hand the control stick with flip-over gun safety trigger. What triumphs had he seen in a cockpit like this? What terrors?

Ben stood on the ladder by his side and listened as Eder explained the controls and gages as he had to newcomers in *Kommando Nowotny*, in the *Eprobungskommando*, in *Jagdgeschwader* 7. His English was totally inadequate for the jargon of aviation, but his enthusiasm was not.

The photographer tried to set up some poses. Could Ben get closer? Lean over some how? He tried, but it did not work. Ben had an idea. He crawled back and twisted into the rear cockpit. It was stripped except for the seat – all the controls and gages had been used to make the front complete. He did not sit, but leaned forward on the console separating the cockpits. Eder stuck his thumb up. Ben grinned and put his up too. Eder smiled. The shutter clicked.

The visit to his old airplane could have been the highlight of Eder's visit, except for the South African Air Force.

Georg-Peter Eder and Ben Drew in the cockpit of one of the few surviving Me 262s.

General Denis Earp was the Chief of Staff for the SAAF, the South African Air Force. He was a combat veteran himself having flown a *Mustang* with Number 2 Squadron, the *Flying Cheetahs*, in Korea. Earp had also been a POW after being shot down in North Korea. He had read about Eder's visit in one of the several articles the South African newspapers had published.

His aide-de-camp telephoned. Would Major Eder and Major Drew care to visit Waterkloof Air Base? 0900, tomorrow? A tour, then luncheon. Business suits were fine. No, no wives; just the men.

The SAAF Memorial sits on the top of a hill on the edge of the air base. Its stark, swooping angles are visible from the Pretoria—Johannesburg Highway and dominate entry to the SAAF's largest base. A full colonel escort met Eder and Ben at the main gate. An official sedan with driver took them on a tour. The flags of the Republics of South Africa and Federal Germany waved from the fenders.

On the flight line, all of Number Three Squadron, the *Wasps*, was assembled in orderly ranks, their *Mirage* fighters lined up behind them. The sedan with Eder at the right window drove slowly past. Men stood at attention, officers saluted, the squadron flag dipped in tribute.

A *Mirage* with a ladder to the cockpit was on display. Orange, white, and blue stripes on the rudder bright on the otherwise brown and green camouflaged jet. The blue body, tan winged wasp of Number Three squadron was in a small circle on the tail. A selected squadron pilot explained the controls and instruments to Eder in fluent German. The *Mirage's* one engine produced as much thrust as three two engined *Messerschmitt 262s*.

General Earp had invited all the generals and most of the colonels of the SAAF to lunch. There were thirty-one high ranking officers at a long table. Earp sat across from Eder and stood to make a brief speech.

"Gentlemen, we are gathered here to honor one of the world's greatest fighter pilots. It matters not at all the color of the uniform he wore or the country he fought for. That is unimportant. What is important is his bravery, skill, dedication, and true professionalism in the air."

After the standing ovation, he presented Eder with a gilt edged plaque in memory of his visit. Another two hours were spent in the bar answering questions. It was late afternoon when Ben and Georg-Peter went home. Eder had tears in his eyes. "Ben, I don't know who you know, but I tell you, my country never did anything like this for me. Never. I thank you from the bottom of my heart."

Pilots hate hospitals. A hospital is everything that flying is not. Hospitals confine and restrict. In a hospital, a pilot no longer has control. The hatred goes beyond the needles and tubes, the hundred humiliations and indignities. In a hospital the sky is gone. Walls become limits. At altitude a pilot's life depends on tubes and mechanical connections, but Oxygen and radio are acceptable. Saline and transfusion are not. A pilot can no longer move with the touch of a control stick. People in white coats direct his every action. Hospitals are antiseptic, cold and white as death. Pilots hate hospitals.

But Ben Drew went willingly to a hospital. His friend had asked him to.

He had gone from South Africa all the way to Wiesbaden, Germany. His friend, Georg-Peter had said to come. It was Cancer. *Krebs* in German – an ugly word in any language. A Cancer that had been eating away at his guts for months. Now he was dying. He wanted to be with Ben Drew.

Ben placed his single bag on the floor and asked the nurse at the admissions desk where Eder's room was. She looked startled, rose from her chair. "*Sind Sie Herr* Drew?"

He said he was.

Expressionless, she asked him to wait, dialed, and spoke rapidly into the telephone.

In two minutes, a tall man strode into the room. He barely paused to look around and went straight to Ben. He wore a stiffly starched, crisply white, long doctor's coat. His white shirt was also starched with a dark necktie drawn up tight so not a fraction of collar showed. He stood straight as though his starched clothes stuck to his skin. One arm was jammed hard into a pocket. He was not smiling.

"Who are you und vhy are you here?" His English was clear with only a trace of accent. He clipped his words precisely.

Ben said his name and that he was there to visit Eder as he stuck out his hand. The *Doktor* was slow to shake hands. When he did his grip was firm and he pumped up and down twice. He did not smile.

"The man you have come to visit is one of the great heroes of our country. Many of the most famous und brave men who served in the *Luftwaffe* have come to see him. Yet he requested that you, an American, a onetime enemy, come to see him. Vhy?"

Ben wondered what to say. This man was obviously important. The admissions nurse was standing stiffly at her desk. Two younger men in white coats stopped their chatter when they saw him and walked gravely to the other door. Another nurse stood quietly against the wall, clipboard in hand, solemn, listening to each word.

"I was also a fighter pilot," said Ben. "Georg-Peter read about a late decoration I received and contacted me through the *Gemeinschaft der JagdFlieger* . We started to correspond. I live in South Africa and invited Mr. and Mrs. Eder to visit. They spent six weeks with my wife and I. We became friends."

"You are still serving in the Air Force?"

Ben smiled. "No, Sir, I was released in 1948."

"You are not here in any official capacity then?"

Ben thought he knew why the *Doktor* was so formal and suspicious. Ben wanted to assure him so he could visit with Eder. "I am only a private citizen. I buy and sell airliners. For awhile I ran an airline in Southwest Africa."

The *Doktor* nodded his head slightly. "I still do not understand. But since it is *Major* Eder's request, you are welcome." Ben noted the use of Eder's thirty year old military rank.

The *Doktor* snapped off orders in rapid German too fast for Ben to follow. The desk nurse sat and started dialing. The younger nurse with the clipboard, stepped closer while writing rapidly. He turned back to Ben. "I haf arranged a cot for you in his room. You may eat in my cafeteria or the room as you wish. It is my pleasure." His expression did not show that he was pleased. "Nursing Sister Schmidt will assist you." He did an about face and marched out of the room.

When the stern *Doktor* left, Sister Schmidt was transformed. Her shoulders relaxed loosening the tautness of her apron front. What had been thin lips parted into a smile that punched dimples in her cheeks. Her face was coyly down while her eyes flirted. Ben was willing to bet that outside the hospital she was quite a swinger.

She put her hand out. "Hi. I'm Helga Schmidt. Don't let *'der Kommandant'* put you off. He can be very nice. Let's get you up to see if *Herr* Eder is awake. I know he's been looking forward to your visit."

"Thank you Sister Schmidt..."

"Helga, please."

"Helga. Your English is very good."

"Tank you. Beside school, my Aunty Emily married a GI and I spend a summer in North Carolina. It was a lot of fun."

"Tell me, that doctor, was he..."

Helga laughed. "Why do you tink ve call him *'der Kommandant'*? He is now the *Chefartz*, the head of this hospital, but he was for many years a *Wehrmacht doktor*. Much time on the Eastern front. The head of a military hospital is titled *Kommandant*. There are rumors, only rumors mind you, that he should have been on trial at Nuremberg. I don't know. It was all so long ago."

So long ago, thought Ben. Young lady, you have no idea. The memory is still fresh and sharp. I wonder what you have been taught. But then, would I have ever imagined in 1944 that the Germans would be our friends? That I would be visiting a *Luftwaffe* ace, a friend, in a hospital in Germany?

They all came. They all came to the hospital to see Georg-Peter Eder. They came to see one of their own. If they were alive, if they had survived the war and combat in the skies over North Africa, Russia, Spain, England, over Germany itself, they came.

The famous ones came. Holders of the Knights Cross of the Iron Cross, with oak leaves, with swords, a few with diamonds, *brillanten*. The men who counted their victories in the hundreds.

Others came. Men who had been scared kids, forced into airplanes they barely understood to fight against an overwhelming enemy. Some had been successful – had shot down Allied airplanes. Most considered success simply to have lived through the experience. Some owed their lives to the man in the hospital bed. His instruction, his counsel as well as his fighting ability. They came in tribute to the life they had shared. Now they had many careers; in business, in the professions. Some retired after the German *Republik* belatedly awarded pensions from wartime service. A few had had careers in the new *Luftwaffe*, flown jet fighters generations removed from their *Schwalbe*. The younger ones were the new Germany. The new divided Germany. The older ones were a link to their national past. A memory never to be forgotten.

They all came. They came and shuffled awkwardly in the antiseptic white of a scrubbed hospital room. They stood nervously and muttered platitudes because they did not know what else to do. They were tough men, trained to war, but now they were frightened. Warriors are frightened in hospital rooms. They were prepared for death tomorrow from the moment they first climbed in a warplane. Their unspoken prayer was – is – if I must go, then make it clean. Make it honorable. Make it fast. Above all, do not make it like this. Not like this man, wasting away, in pain, dragging through the last of life. This man, our friend, *unser Kamerad*, one of us.

Years had passed. The invulnerability of youth had gone away slowly but surely. They all knew they were to die, not tomorrow in glory, in combat, but like this. So they shuffled and did not know what to say. Ben was there for them all. The looks and reactions on first introductions went from surprise, to wonder, to reserve or friendly, but always to welcome. Ben Drew was a diversion. Someone to look at besides the man dying in bed. They told the old stories. The tales from the flight line, the hangar, the officers' club, the *Kasino*. They told them in English, fluent or fractured, in German and English swirled and confused, they told them in gestures, some words, and the universal waving hands of pilots. They had much in common.

There was an appropriateness in both Georg-Peter Eder and Urban L. Drew ending their service as majors. A comfortable middle rank. Neither had wanted a military career. Neither had stayed long after the shooting stopped. Both had done what they had to do. They had both defended their country when it went to war. They had not worried about the politics or deeper meanings of the conflict. They were in the right and they would risk their lives for victory. That they were on opposing sides was now insignificant. They were more alike than different. They were warriors. They understood each other in a way no other person ever could.

Ben had to leave eventually. It was difficult and easy. Difficult because his friend would be alone in the long hours of the night. Easy because they had established their peace. They had said goodbye. Ben went back to his house on Waterkloof Ridge in South Africa.

A week later, the telephone rang. Lynette answered. It was Eder. She stayed on the line as Ben picked up the extension in case she needed to translate. It was not necessary. Eder said, "Ben, I love you. *Horrido.*"

Four days later he died.

Chapter Notes

8. *Leipheim*:
The *Gigant* as a glider went from being the Me263 to the Me321. 50 Me321As were built and 100 dual control Me321Bs. The huge glider was used, but saw no major actions – it was too late for Stalingrad. The tow problem was never solved satisfactorily, and French *Gnome-Rhone* engines were installed. Four engines were not enough and six became standard. The powered *Gigant* was designated the Me323 and 201 were built. The flight controls were servo-mechanical and the co-pilot's main job was trimming. The flight mechanics' stations inside of each wing had an upper surface hatch. For defense, the *Gigant* had more machine guns than a B-17.

9. *Bartow*:
One of Drew's students was Dale Spencer who became the top scorer of the 361st Group with ten destroyed in the air.
Another student was James Jabara who, during the Korean War, became America's first jet ace by destroying fifteen MiG 15s.
The city of Tallahassee grew and spread to include Dale Mabrey Field. Students at Florida State University would illegally race their cars on the old runways.

10. *Bottisham*:
275th Squadron was not called the "Yellowjackets" until October of 1944.

12. *Lisieaux:*

The problems with the PSP was one of the main reasons the 361st moved to Little Walden when they had a chance. The previous B-26 Bomb wing had moved to the Continent and their base with concrete runways was available.

Perhaps because of the easily removed PSP, almost no evidence of Bottisham as an airbase exists today, according to those who make a study of such things. The strongest connection to the war years are a plaque in the local church and a street in the village named for Colonel Christian.

15. *Cambridgeshire:*

Mr. Jan Buskens of Kraainem, Belgium, wrote the author as follows:

When you look carefully at good color pictures you will see that two of the "Bottisham Four" have dark blue paint on the tail and upper fuselage: E2*C, "Lou IV", and E2*A, "Skybouncer".

As for Ben Drew being there and none of the group's veterans remembering blue painted *Mustangs*, they probably did not pay attention to camouflage colors as they had other things on their minds. The rule was olive drab and not so many aircraft were painted blue and then only for a short time. The blue was a dark shade and not that prominent.

I wrote to Roger Freeman (aviation historian) and he assured me there were blue painted *Mustangs* in the 361st FG. He mentions color slides in the archives and first hand reports. One person who was there was Michael Bowyer who was a spotter and therefore a more reliable observer of markings and color. A portion of his article in *Airfix Magazine* is enclosed.

From *Airfix Magazine*, October 1979:

My most vivid memory of the P-51s will always date from July 9, 1944. Here at hand was a clutch of three P-51s natural finished at a time when about half the USAAF aircraft in Britain had shed camouflage. These were among those Bottisham Mustangs that had acquired a most superb blue upper decking to wings and fuselage. The colour was what I described in my diary as "really Royal Blue". I noted that it was not desecrated by the addition of invasion stripes. A generous American led me to E9*O, a then new P-51D already resplendent in the new blue scheme.

16. *Germany:*

Early in the war, Eder had met a French woman, fallen in love, and understood that they would be formally engaged. The woman was the daughter of Admiral Darlan, later famous as the commander of French Forces in North Africa. Admiral Darlan swore that, "No daughter of mine will ever marry a *Luftwaffe* pilot."

19. *The English Channel:*

In 1996, a Frenchman, Laurent Wiart, discovered Colonel Christian's grave in a World War One British cemetery. Fascinated by the 1944 date on the marker, he pursued the story. Colonel Christian had apparently spent a day or two in a German military hospital before dying of his injuries. A possible reason for confusion about his nationality was his flight gear. Typical of pilots who arrived in England in 1943, Colonel Christian wore an RAF flight suit, helmet and goggles.

His daughter turned down the US military's offer to have his remains moved to Arlington National Cemetery. She decided it was fitting to "let him remain where he fell." Lou Ellen Loving did go to France to see the grave site and to modern Bottisham where, in a moving ceremony, she helped dedicate a street named in her father's honor. Appropriately, *Thomas Christian Way* is located on the site of the 361 Group's old living area.

20. *Witmund:*

Excerpts from letter from Bernard Redden, Secretary/Editor of 361st Fighter Group Assoc., November, 1998:

I can assure you that the *Marie* whose name was painted on E2-X was the girl who would become my wife after the war, You see, we of the ground crew only let the pilots believe it was their plane, and so allowed them to personalize it as regulations permitted.

However, the aircraft was assigned to a ground crew, after which a pilot was assigned to fly it. That is why many aircraft bore the names of two members of the opposite sex. "Isabel-Miss Margie", "Geraldine-Marge", "Little Moke-Christine", "Yvonne-Marie", "Vicki-Belle" and "Ruthie-Bev" are a few that come to mind.

I was not the crew chief on Kemp's plane. That distinction goes to S/Sgt. Ted W. Coker for whom I was assistant crew chief for my entire stay in the ETO. As far as I know, Vern Davis was assistant crew chief to S/Sgt. Tony Wnek on the aircraft E2-N "Little Snitz" which was Lt. Alton Snyder's personal plane. It could be that Ben flew that aircraft on occasion. Pilots were assigned to fly different planes if their own was not available. Vern and I were in different flights, so it would be rare that we worked on the same aircraft; not impossible, mind you, for on the night of June 5th, 1944, we scrambled around to wherever we were needed to get those invasion stripes painted on the planes.

24. *Baltic Sea*:

There is a conflict in the dates of the final *Frantic* shuttle mission and Drew's flight over the Baltic on September 11, 1944. The shuttle missions did last several days, so Drew's recollection that it was a *Frantic* he had escorted may be correct.

Another development on who sank the only flyable BV238 appeared in an article "Former enemies are brought together by destroyed aircraft" in the *San Diego Union Tribune*. John Wilkens, a staff writer, brought Drew and Hans Amtmann together on April 21, 1997. Amtmann claims it could not have been Drew's flight, but has no firm evidence for who did sink the flying boat. Any further information is solicited by the author.

28. *Rheine*

McCandliss carried pepper because he had read in a WW I flying story that pepper would make a dog lose its sense of smell. He thought it would be useful if he was trying to evade and search dogs were being used in the hunt.

In a rare considerate move, the USAAF designated certain training bases as primarily for married students. Dale Mawbrey Field was one of these so Virginia McCandliss did not have to chase around the country or be separated from her new husband while he was in training.

29. *Achmer*:
The third Me262 crashing because of running over ejected cartridges is the author's speculation. A *Luftwaffe* source says the tires were shot out by the *Mustangs*. Neither Drew nor McCandliss saw a third Me262, much less shot at one. Eder told Drew that the third jet did swerve off the runway, but did not say why.

31. *Christmas:*
Eder was 5'6" tall. At a meeting of the "Rebel" *Luftwaffe* aces with Göring, in January, 1945, Göring called them cowards, and said women and children would die because they were afraid to close with the bombers. General Galland took off his Knights Cross, threw it at Göring's feet and stalked from room. Eder stood up and said, "*Herr Reichsmarschall*, I have no argument with you calling me a coward. You can call me anything you want. But you will never call my dead comrades cowards. I demand a retraction."

After a long pause, *Reichsmarschall* Göring said to the insubordinate Captain, "Eder, for a little man you have a big mouth." There were no repercussions.

33. *Europe:*
Eder wound up in the interrogation center at Ely in Britain. The Germans called it Stalag 13 in ironic parody of where Allied prisoners had been kept. His treatment was brutal and included almost daily beatings. A Red Cross Major on an inspection tour, found out and asked

Eder why he didn't tell the British what they wanted to know. Eder responded, "Major, what did they tell you to say when your country lost the war?"

To get him out, the Major briefed Eder on how a schizophrenic would act. In Africa, Eder told Drew, "I had to go mad for a couple of days." He was transferred to an American military hospital in Germany and released. The sad treatment was why he never set foot in England or America and ignored the language.

During his London days, Drew was at dinner with a Member of Parliament, who was an RAF veteran and told Eder's story. The MP at first denied it, but when pressed, his wife asked him to, "think again", and had him check the records he had access to as an MP. A month later, the MP telephoned Drew and said, "I apologize, we did torture German prisoners after all."

Glossary

A problem with glossaries is just how much to include. The following are some of the words readers of the rough manuscript questioned. This glossary should also save trips to the dictionary, if indeed, some of the jargon peculiar to military aviation can even be found there.

BLACKMEN—the mechanics, armorers and other ground staff of the Luftwaffe wore a standard issue coverall that was black, hence the term.

GEMEINSCHAFT DER JAGDFLIEGER – a fraternal and professional society of German fighter pilots from 1914 to the present.

GERMAN RANKS—the lower four officer ranks, equivalent to U.S. 2nd Lieutenant., 1st Lt., Captain and Major, were *Leutnant, Oberleutnant, Hauptmann,* and *Major. Major,* although spelled the same as in English is pronounced Mai-yor.

HONORIFICS—the *Luftwaffe* used a series of titles for unit commanders that were independent of actual military rank. (Much like the "Captain" of a ship is not necessarily a *Captain* in rank.) The commanding officer of a *Staffel* was called *Kapitän;* a *Gruppe,* a *Kommandeur;* and a *Geschwader,* a *Kommodore.* Their staffs were called *Stab* and flew as a small unit of their own.

KRIEGIE—in German, Prisoners of War were *Kriegsgefangenen*. The POW's themselves naturally shortened this to something pronounceable.

LATRINE- easy enough; it is the army term for bathroom.

LEAD/LEAD/LED – a favorite of aviation writers. To shoot at a moving target, one must aim in front to allow for the bullets' time of flight. This is leading the target. The bullets are made of lead. More than one airplane needs a leader for the flight. The past tense of lead is led.

LOUIE- American army slang for Lieutenant. There were "first louies" and "second louies". A Lieutenant-Colonel was sometimes called a "light" colonel as opposed to a "full" or "bird" colonel.

MAE WEST—the emergency flotation equipment worn around the neck and over an airman's chest was named after the buxom movie actress because of how one looked when the equipment was inflated. Supposedly, Miss West was flattered when she learned this.

ME—Although purists will scream, I used this throughout as the abbreviation for the Messerschmitt designed fighter, the 109. Officially it was the Bf 109. Bf is the abbreviation for the Bavarian Airplane works , *Bavarische Flugzeugwerke*. After factories were dispersed and several manufacturers were building one design, the German high command did what the Soviet Union had been doing for years and designated aircraft by their designer. Thus the *Schwalbe* was officially a Messerschmitt airplane; the Me 262. Most people are familiar with the slightly sinister sound of the name Messerschmitt, therefore Me109. Also the American pilots of the time said "Messerschmitt" or "ME".

PIPPER—the dot in the center of an optical (also called a reflector) gunsight. The equivalent of the cross hairs of the older, metal sight. When the lead computing sight was developed, the pipper was the dot that showed the aimimg point. Hence, the modern brag after a practice fight that your opponent was suffering from "pipper burn".

P.S.P. – Pierced Steel Planking. Also called Marston Matting. Steel panels that interconnectted to quickly make a hard surface runway.

RETICLE—also part of a reflector gun or bombsight. The reticle is the complete illuminated image which includes the pipper, rings to estimate range, and various vertical, horizontal and angle indicators.

REVETMENT- a U-shaped fortification to protect vehicles, equipment or aircraft from bomb or artillery shrapnel. Sometimes of masonry or sandbag construction, but usually just mounds of dirt pushed into position.

TACTICAL ORGANIZATION—from small to large, in English and German: (numbers from squadron / staffel and up varied)

Element / *Rotte*	2 airplanes
Flight / *Schwarm*	4 airplanes
Squadron / *Staffel*	16-20 airplanes
Group / *Gruppe*	60-70 airplanes
Wing / *Geschwader*	200-250 airplanes

Katzenjammer Kids

The *Katzenjammer Kids* was a newspaper cartoon strip that was especially popular throughout World War Two. The multiple panel, Sunday cartoon featured characters who spoke with bizarre German dialects and made jokes based on the stupid, elaborate schemes of naïve immigrants. Slapstick was heavily used and episodes usually ended in a spanking for the kids. It was perfect for generating anti-German sentiment.

The *Katzenjammer Kids* was started by Rudolph Dirks, himself a German immigrant, in 1897. He had an argument with Hearst and left that chain of papers to start his own strip with the same format. However, a court order forbid him from using the original name. Dirks called his strip *Hans and Fritz*, but changed it to *The Captain and the Kids* during World War One so it sounded less German. The *Katzenjammer Kids* continued with different artists for the Hearst papers. Fourteen animated cartoons appeared 1938-39.

The major characters were *der Captain, Momma, der Perfessor* and two mischievous boys, the *Katzenjammer Kids*. All the characters spoke with laughably heavy German accents. The Kids were always playing some prank which backfired and resulted in them being spanked. The Kids were usually either wide-eyed with innocent wonder or smiling so hard they had no eyes.

In German, *Katzenjammer* is the word for an alcoholic hangover.

Index

361 Fighter Group, 124
375 Fighter Squadron, 55, 73, 78, 92, 177, 229
376 Fighter Squadron, 100
3 Bomb Division, 128
4 Fighter Group, 72-73
414 Fighter Squadron, 187, 206, 210
448 Bomb Group, 124
54 Fighter Group, 42
56 Fighter Group , 42
56 Fighter Squadron, 42
Achmer, Germany, 1, 147, 152, 170-177, 180, 210, 224, 227, 233, 247
Armsby, Sherman Lt., 55, 73
Armstrong, Col., 221
AT-6, North American *Texan,* 28, 188, 190
Bain, Robert 2Lt, 100
Ball, Bobby, *Detroit News* , 223
Bartow, Florida, 34, 42
Beder, 110, 125
Blakeslee, Colonel , 73,130, 147
Bley, *Oberleutnant,* 170-174, 249

Blohm and Voss BV222, *Viking,* 132,228
Blohm and Voss, BV238 , 133,228, 246
Bluenthal Airfield, Wilmington, NC, 191, 193, 196
Bottisham Cambridgeshire, England, 43, 50-60, 69-79, 96-100, 105, 116, 119, 124, 128, 136, 145, 155, 244-245
C-47, Douglas, *Dakota,* 135-136, 144
Chartres, France, 56, 78, 92, 94, 96, 180
Christian, Colonel Thomas J.J., Jr, 52-57, 63, 76-79, 97-101, 227, 244, 245
Christian, Lou, 226, 227, 245
Cochrane, Colonel *Flip,* 38
Cowell, Captain, 142-143
Crandell, Lt. *Jack* , 60, 65
Cruikshank, Sergeant, 73, 120
Cumbaa, Capt. Noel, 22, 23
Cummins, Major, 55, 65, 92, 128, 148

Dauntless, Douglas A-24 (Navy SBD), 36
Davis, Vernon, Staff Sergeant, 107, 117, 246
Detroit, Michigan, 3-7, 118, 186, 220
Doolittle, General, USAAF, 156
Drew, Earl, 3, 5, 186, 190, 224
Drew, Mrs. Lynette (Cronje), 224, 242
Drew, Mrs. Mary (Breitenstern), 224
Drew, Mrs. Olive, 4, 122, 185
Dunnigan, Francis Xavier, 22-24
Earp, General Denis, SAAF, 236
Eder, Georg-Peter, xi, 83-88, 170-176, 183-196, 233-242, 245, 247-248
Emlaw, Dr. Maynard, 55, 106
Engstrom, 101
Eprobungskommando, 235
Flying Fortress, Boeing B-17, 81-85, 150, 196-199
Focke-Wulf FW190, 65, 72, 72, 94, 166, 180
Freeman, Major, 56
Galland, *General, Luftwaffe*, 171, 174, 247
Glankler, Captain Francis *Frank*, 55, 76-79, 99, 110, 227
Gourock, Glasgow, Scotland, 47, 177

Guyckeson, Captain John, 56
Hamm, Germany, 139
Harker, Colonel Ward, 34, 38
Heinkel, He111, 30, 131, 180
Helldiver, Curtis A-25 (Navy SB2C), 36
Houston, Captain Larry, 50-52, 73, 132, 136
Iwo Jima, 192, 205-209, 211-215
Jagdgeschwader 7, 7, 235
Johnson, Martin, 55, 63-71, 79, 99
Junkers Ju52, 30, 60
Katzenjammer, 72, 75, 93, 108, 119, 1247, 129, 142, 180, 219, 226, 253
Keller, *General, Luftwaffe,* 174-175
Kelly, Governor of Michigan, 221
Kemp, Mrs Betty Lee, 104, 118
Kemp, William *Billy,* 36-41, 44, 48-62, 66, 72-75, 78-80, 92-96, 102-110, 118, 120-121, 128, 142, 148, 179-180, 218
Kingsbury, USS, 203-204
Knupp, Lt. *Danny*, 129, 144
Kobert, *Leutnant,* 86, 166, 171, 249
Kommando Nowotny, 1, 152, 171-175, 235
Kruzel, LtCol. *Joe,* 63, 65, 99, 118, 149, 177-179, 191, 227
Lake Schall, Germany, 132
Leipheim, Germany, 31
Leuther, 171, 173

Liberator, Consolidated B-24, 126, 150
Lightning, Lockheed P-38, 111, 175
Lisieaux, France, 63
Little Walden, England, 122, 132, 177
Loughead, John, 188
Malden, Missouri, 244
Marianna, Florida, 28
Mayer, Egon, 83
McCandliss, Robert, vi, 2, 143-146, 152-154, 158-169, 184-185, 196-200, 226, 247
McCandliss, Virginia (Goodall), 142, 185, 247
McCoppin, William, 55, 150-152, 156, 218, 224, 227
Merritt, LtCol. George, 56
Messerschmitt Me110 *Zerstörer*, 172
Messerschmitt Me262 *Schwalbe*, 1, 31-33, 140-143, 152-156, 170-176, 183, 196, 229, 234, 236, 247
Messerschmitt Me263 *Gigant*, 30
Messerschmitt Me109, 64, 68, 86, 92, 125, 180
Montgomery, Alabama, 8
Moore, Lt. Charles, 177
Mosquito, DeHaviland, 91
Murdoch, LtCol. *Mooch-Head*, 215

Mustang, North American A-36, 34
Narvis, Lt., 55, 129, 177
Nowotny Major Walter, *Luftwaffe*, 171, 175
Orr, Vernon, Secretary of Air Force, 230, 231
Patton, General George, USA, 134, 137
Pretoria, South Africa, 225, 228-234
Queen Elizabeth, Cunard Liner, 43-47
Rainey, 55, 101
Regan, Harold, 187, 191, 209-213
Rheine, Germany, 158, 162, 172
Rogers, William *Billy*, 55, 58, 132-133, 227
Rossbach, Hans, historian, 233
Rostock, Germany, 79, 109, 180
Rowlett, Captain Bruce *Red*, 55, 76, 79, 149, 155, 177, 227
Russel, *Oberfähnreich*, 172-173
Saipan, 204, 214-216
Seppala, Major Leslie, 28-29
Sigler, Governor of Michigan, 222
Spaatz, General USAAF, 107
Spitfire, Supermarine, 60-71
Stearman Pt-19, 12-21
Steffy, Capt, 221
Tallahassee, Florida, 41, 43, 159, 243

Thorne, Col. *Hank*, 191-194, 205, 207, 215
Thunderbolt, Republic P-47, 98, 100, 191, 207, 211, 213
Toussus-Le Noble, France, 56, 59
Travis, Lee, 132, 134-136
Troika-Schlepp, 30-31
Tshombe, Moise, 225
Tuscaloosa, Alabama., 11, 14, 19, 22
Vultee, Vultee BT-13, 25
Wade, Jake, 187, 18, 191
Wendel, *Flugkapitain* Fritz, 32
Wiesbaden, Germany, 237
Witmund, Germany, 100, 246
Wood, 2Lt. Leonard, 92-96, 226
Wright, 1Lt. Robert, 55
Zemke, Col. Hubert *Hub*, 43, 147, 197
Zieske, 101

About the Author

R.R. "Boom" Powell was a career U.S. Navy officer who flew from carrier decks for sixteen years before starting to write about aviation. His thirty-seven years as a pilot and especially his combat experience, give this biography of a fighter ace an immediacy and familiarity not found in ordinary histories. Powell has written for several magazines and has a novel with the same setting as the Drew saga in work as well as a *Great War* flying tale. He flies Boeing 747 freighters for an international airline when he is not writing or soaring in his Libelle.

Please send historical corrections, additions or comments to:

Robert R. Powell

5344 Reasor Court

Virginia Beach, VA 23464-2422

Fax: 757-523-9139

e-mail: *Vigihawk@aol.com*

About the Artist

Troy White, an artist well-recognized for his dramatic and colorful aviation paintings, is also a pilot and skydiver of over twenty years. He prides himself on creating aviation scenes which are both eye-catching works of art and accurate representations of moments in history. Troy currently specializes in oil paintings of aircraft from the World War II and Korean War eras.

Cover Painting:

Ben Drew goes one-on-one in the dogfight described in the chapter titled *Rostock*. The original oil on canvas painting "The Katzenjammer Kid" by Troy White is 44 "x34".

Original artwork, prints and graphics are available from:

STARDUST STUDIOS

2425 Nectarine Road

DeLand, FL 32724

386-738-3142 *phone & fax*

e-mail: troy@totcon.com or troy@starduststudios.com

0-595-20638-7

Printed in the United States
49506LVS00005B/1-102